M000197933

Especially For:

_____

From:

_____

Date:

_____

The
Woman's Secret
of a
Happy Life

3-MINUTE DEVOTIONS

Inspired by the Beloved Classic by
Hannah Whitall Smith

Donna K. Maltese

BARBOUR BOOKS
An Imprint of Barbour Publishing, Inc.

© 2020 by Barbour Publishing, Inc.

ISBN 978-1-64352-702-4

Member of the
Evangelical Christian
Publishers Association

Printed in the United States of America.

Want the Secret to a Happy Life?

These devotions were written especially for those moments when you need a little reminder that every single day can be filled with happiness. Just three tiny minutes is all you'll need to refresh and revitalize your spirit.

- Minute 1: Read the day's Bible verse and reflect on its meaning.

- Minute 2: Read the devotional and think about its application for your life.

- Minute 3: Pray.

Although these devotions aren't meant as a tool for deep Bible study, they can be a touch point to keep you grounded and focused on God, the Giver of joy. May every moment you spend with this book be a blessing!

A Deep Happiness

God's power is working in us....
Our hearts ache, but we always have joy.
2 CORINTHIANS 6:7, 10 NLT

Christians have access to a deep happiness, one not contingent on our earthly situation. It's based on a calm assurance that *in spite of* what's happening around us, we're trusting in Jesus, certain that the Holy Spirit is with us and that God will work all things out for our good. It's about rising above the trials and tribulations of this life to find that unspeakable happiness, that calmness, that sweet assurance in knowing that through flood and fire, the Lord's light is upon us.

God, help me rise above the trials of this
life to find Your unspeakable happiness,
that calmness of You dwelling within me.

Choose Joy

In Your presence is abundant joy;
in Your right hand are eternal pleasures.
PSALM 16:11 HCSB

You have the choice to be joyful or fearful, to hand your burdens over to Jesus or keep them firmly in your white-knuckled grip, to feel a growing hopelessness and desperation or experience a deep sense of peace. It's a choice you make each and every moment of every day, regardless of your circumstances. This does not mean plastering a fake smile on your face but rather learning to be *joyful* instead of *woeful*. Unlike the "worldlings," who allow their emotions to rise and fall like the stock market, we Christians should abide in the love and joy of Christ, which is ours for the taking.

Lord God, today I choose joy. Make Your
presence known to me in this moment.

Victory Within and Without

We wait for the LORD. He is our help
and our shield. In him our hearts
find joy. In his holy name we trust.
PSALM 33:20-21 GW

Take to heart every line of God's truth. Claim each promise as your very own. Believe that your life may be enriched by incorporating His truths into your experiences. While you work toward this, be patient with yourself. It takes time to reconstruct and readjust your attitude to life, God, yourself, and your surroundings. But never give up. God has a wonderful plan for your life. He is not only abiding with you on your inward journey but will give you victory without as well.

Lord, help me claim every word of
Your truth as my very own. Amen.

Let Go and Let God

*Sarah said, "God has brought me laughter, and
everyone who hears about this will laugh with me."*
GENESIS 21:6 GW

This life in Christ is to be lived to the fullest, not
in partial victories and agonizing defeats. We are
not to live as "Hagars," slaves to sin, but instead as
free women like Sarah. Once she trusted God to deliver as promised, He brought her laughter. Once
Sarah banished fear and doubt, once she stopped
trying to fix things herself, once she "let go and
let God," His promises became her reality, and she
was overjoyed!

*Help me make Your promises to me become
my reality, Lord, by banishing fear and doubt
and leaving all in Your capable hands.*

Saved!

God made you alive with Christ, for he forgave all our sins. He canceled the record of the charges against us and took it away by nailing it to the cross.

COLOSSIANS 2:13–14 NLT

Christians can be joyful because we are saved—not because we don't sin. We still miss the mark. But we can find joy in knowing that our debt for sin has been paid in full through the death of Jesus on the cross.

We rejoice because that sin, the obstacle standing between us and God, has been expunged from our record. "And in addition to everything else, we are happy because God sent our Lord Jesus Christ to make peace with us" (Romans 5:11 CEV).

Thank You, Lord, for the joy of Your forgiveness!

More than Conquerors

*I want you to know about the great and mighty
power that God has for us followers. It is the same
wonderful power he used when he raised Christ from
death and let him sit at his right side in heaven.*

EPHESIANS 1:19–20 CEV

We, as Christ followers, have "the same wonderful power" of the One who calmed the sea and stopped the wind. And that all we need to do to access that mighty power is to let Christ live through us, to trust Him with our lives, to honor Him with our words. We can stop cowering and instead understand that "we are more than conquerors and gain a surpassing victory through Him Who loved us" (Romans 8:37 AMPC).

....

*I praise You, Lord, for the gift of the power
of the One who calmed the seas. Amen.*

The Promise of Joy

God is on our side.
ROMANS 8:31 AMPC

Through thick and thin, God is on our side. And Jesus "is able always to save those who come to God through him because he always lives, asking God to help them" (Hebrews 7:25 NCV). So we never need to fear at any time! That alone should bring joy and peace into our hearts!

We know that in Jesus we are saved, we have access to power, and we are more than conquerors. Where then does an expectation or promise of joy come in? It comes in Christ! It comes in trusting Him, applying His Word to our lives, and living out our faith.

*Help me trust You more and more
each day, Lord. Amen.*

Abba God

*Because we are his children, God has
sent the Spirit of his Son into our hearts,
prompting us to call out, "Abba, Father."*
GALATIANS 4:6 NLT

God doesn't promise that we won't have trials. We might lose a job, a house, a husband, a child; we'll have sickness, dashed hopes, and unmet expectations. Jesus Himself was disappointed with people at times, including His own disciples. He displayed His anger with the money changers and suffered His share of loss. But He also enjoyed a deep relationship with Father God. Like Jesus, we too are children of God, and because we are His, He sent Jesus' Spirit into our hearts. By following in Jesus' steps, we can have the same joyous relationship with Abba God.

....

Jesus, I plan to follow in Your steps. Amen.

The Joy of His Presence

*There is a friend who sticks
closer than a brother.*

PROVERBS 18:24 NKJV

In Christ we have a good friend, a "big brother" who can and will defend us against all enemies, look out for us, size up our situations, and advise us. He loves us like no other, shielding us from evil, taking on all challengers, gladly bearing our burdens. When others disappoint, discourage, depress, or desert us, He stands by our side. He watches over us as we sleep, guarding the gates. What joy His constant presence gives us! But we must be *aware* of His presence—within and without, above and below, to the right and the left.

*In this moment, make me aware
of Your presence, Lord. Amen.*

From Tears to Tango

You have changed my sobbing into dancing.
You have removed my sackcloth and
clothed me with joy so that my soul may
praise you with music and not be silent.
PSALM 30:11–12 GW

Because of Jesus' sacrifice, we can call our Father God *Abba*! And we can be assured of the Holy Spirit's comfort and guidance. So, tell your Brother Jesus all your troubles, including sins. Tell Him you want to do better. Call on Christ's death-defying power. Count on God's protection. Follow the Holy Spirit's guidance. Sing a new song of joy unto the Lord who sees you as His dear daughter. Dance in celebration of Christ's saving grace and power.

In my joy, I sing a new song, I dance
a new dance, in praise of You, Jesus.

Tap into Life-Giving Water

No one will take your
joy away from you.
JOHN 16:22 NASB

Remember that no one can take your joy. Refuse to be like Hagar, sitting down in the midst of your troubles, sobbing, allowing the weight of the world's woes to oppress you. Just like He called Hagar, God is calling you: " 'Don't be afraid!' . . . God opened her eyes. Then she saw a well. She filled the container with water" (Genesis 21:17, 19 GW). God is and always will be with you. Don't let your faith dry up. Run to His well and tap into His life-giving water.

Buoy my faith, Lord, with Your life-giving water.
Drench me in Your presence. Amen.

Vessels of Use

*Each of you is now a new person. You are
becoming more and more like your Creator,
and you will understand him better.*
COLOSSIANS 3:10 CEV

In regard to the subject of God transforming us into the image of His Son Jesus Christ, there are two sides—God's side and woman's side. Simply put, God's role is to work and ours is to trust that He's doing it. We have already been delivered from the danger of sin. Now God works to transform us into vessels He can use. As Isaiah said, "O LORD, You are our Father; we are the clay, and You our Potter; and all we are the work of Your hand" (Isaiah 64:8 NKJV).

*Work within me, Lord, to make me
a vessel You can use. Amen.*

Shaped by God's Hands

If you keep yourself pure, you will be a special utensil for honorable use. . .ready for the Master to use you for every good work.
2 TIMOTHY 2:21 NLT

God has given us His Word to live by. He has given us the power of prayer. He has told us that He loves us. And now we are to be further shaped—by His transforming power—from lumps of clay into vessels He can use.

We have been pulled up out of the miry clay pit and put into His hands. Overjoyed at our coming to Him, God begins to shift our shapes, to pull us apart, to knead us, to mold us. Our role is to remain still, patient, and pliable.

*I lift myself up to You, Lord,
for You to shape as You will. Amen.*

Yielded Up

*Present your bodies a living and holy
sacrifice, acceptable to God, which is
your spiritual service of worship.*

ROMANS 12:1 NASB

God puts His clay upon the wheel, spinning us,
forming us, continually turning us until He is sat-
isfied with our new shapes, and then He smooths
us down. We're put into the furnace and baked until we're exactly what He envisioned us to be. As
clay, we're not expected to do the Potter's work but
simply to yield ourselves up to Him. In order to
trust the Potter to do with us what He will, we must
firmly believe in Him and the process. We must not
doubt or lose focus.

*I believe in You, Lord. I yield
myself up to You! Amen.*

A Case of Obstruction

When Peter saw the wind and the waves,
he became afraid and began to sink.
He shouted, "Lord, save me!"

MATTHEW 14:30 NCV

When we step out of the boat and onto the water to head to Jesus' side, we are putting ourselves in His hands. If we look away from Him and turn our focus to the wind and waves, we are no longer trusting in Jesus. And then, like Peter, we begin to sink. It's as if we have taken ourselves out of the Potter's hands and retreated back into our clay pits. No longer surrendering ourselves to the Potter's skill, we obstruct the work of the master Creator and will remain lumps of clay instead of blossoming into the beautiful vessels He intended.

Help me, Lord, to keep my focus on You! Amen.

The Bane of Unbelief

He did not many mighty works
there because of their unbelief.

MATTHEW 13:58 KJV

When there's no faith in God, there's no trust and no transforming work can happen. *Matthew Henry's Commentary* says Jesus' hometown citizens' lack of belief did, "in effect, tie [Jesus'] hands . . . . Unbelief is the great obstruction to Christ's favours. So that if mighty works be not wrought in us, it is not for want of power or grace in Christ, but for want of faith in us." God forbid we should be found wanting and remain lumps of clay. Or that we miss out on what grand plans God has in store for us because we've sunk down into the dark and deep blue sea!

Increase my faith, Lord, so I may
be transformed in You! Amen.

Only Believe

Is any thing too hard for the LORD?
GENESIS 18:14 KJV

When Jairus, one of the rulers of the synagogue, came to Jesus, he was filled with faith and begged Jesus to heal his young daughter, who was dying. Jesus agreed to do so. As He walked with Jairus toward the ruler's home, some people came from the house, saying, "Your daughter is dead. Why trouble the Teacher any further?" (Mark 5:35 NKJV). But Jesus reassured Jairus with some of the sweetest words found in any language: "Do not be afraid; only believe" (Mark 5:36 NKJV).

....

*Lord, help me to not fear
but only believe! Amen.*

God's Goodness

I would have lost heart, unless I had
believed that I would see the goodness
of the LORD in the land of the living.
PSALM 27:13 NKJV

By the time Jesus got to Jairus's house, a myriad of mourners was there, weeping and wailing. When Jesus told them, "The child is not dead, but sleeping" (Mark 5:39 NKJV), they merely laughed at Him.

So Jesus had them all driven out of the house. Taking with Him Peter, James, and John as well as the child's parents, He went to the little girl's bedside and ordered her to rise. That instant, she got up and began walking around.

What an awesome example of how Jesus works when we believe!

I believe, Lord, that I will see
Your goodness! Amen.

In His Hands

God began doing a good work in you, and I
am sure he will continue it until it is finished.

PHILIPPIANS 1:6 NCV

Hannah Whitall Smith wrote, "All that we claim, then, in this life of sanctification is that by an act of faith we put ourselves into the hands of the Lord, for Him to work in us all the good pleasure of His will, and then, by a continuous exercise of faith, keep ourselves there."

We lumps of clay will not be transformed into vessels overnight. It'll take many spins of the Potter's wheel. But we can rest assured that we're safer in His hands than in a deep, dark pit; and although we may experience growing pains, we'll someday be mature Christians, energized and transformed by the Holy Spirit.

I'm in Your hands, Lord.

Faith versus Efforts

People won't receive God's approval because
of their own efforts. . . . Christ came so that we
could receive God's approval by faith.

GALATIANS 2:16, 3:24 GW

Sarah took herself out of God's hands when she became impatient while waiting to see His promise come to pass. She believed God needed *her* to provide the solution.

May we not be so bold and impatient as Sarah but humble ourselves and allow God time to work us into shapely vessels for Him. And although it is God who is actually doing the work of transformation as we yield ourselves to Him, we are to keep up our faith and believe that He is indeed doing so.

I yield myself to You, Lord.
Work in me Your will and way.

The One Thing

"One thing is needed, and Mary has chosen that good part, which will not be taken away from her."

LUKE 10:42 NKJV

To shore up our trust in God, we can turn to His Word and embed it in our hearts. We can lift our faith by practicing prayer and find ourselves buoyed by remaining in His presence.

Instead of being like Martha, who was "worried and troubled about many things," and "distracted with much serving," we can, like Mary, set ourselves down at Jesus' feet, listening to His every word—the "one thing" needed (Luke 10:40–42 NKJV). When we do so, Jesus will commend each of us because we have "chosen that good part, which will not be taken away" (Luke 10:42 NKJV).

Speak, Lord. I'm listening.

No Stress, No Mess

*In our spiritual nature, faith causes us to
wait eagerly for the confidence that comes
with God's approval.... What matters is a
faith that expresses itself through love....
What matters is being a new creation.*

GALATIANS 5:5-6, 6:15 GW

We need not stress ourselves out with trying to help
God transform us. That's like the batter attempting
to help the baker make it into a cake. It just doesn't
happen. All the batter can do is keep on trusting
and surrendering to the baker. We also need not
try to tell our Creator what we think we should be
and do. In effect, it's out of our hands and in God's.
And thank God for that! It takes all the pressure off
because the stress to perform is removed.

*I'm trusting and surrendering to You,
Lord. Mold me as You will!*

Truly Believe

With God's help, we will do mighty things.
PSALM 60:12 NLT

With our Lord as our eternal master designer, with our ongoing surrender, with our power of belief, with our patient awaiting of His working, we can be assured that God is shaping us into amazing, confident, expectant, joy-filled women. There's no telling what feats He is designing us to perform.

And our part is to merely trust, to surrender, and to follow Christ's injunction: "Do not be seized with alarm and struck with fear; only keep on believing" (Mark 5:36 AMPC). For when we truly believe, we can accomplish the seemingly impossible!

*I believe, Lord! Shape me
into a joy-filled woman!*

Childlike Trust and Faith

*"I tell you the truth, you must accept
the kingdom of God as if you were a
little child, or you will never enter it."*

MARK 10:15 NCV

Unlike the usual Christian experience, in which we believe and have been saved but do not exhibit Christlikeness, the so-called higher Christian life is described in the Bible as one of continual rest in Jesus, of peace that surpasses all understanding. It's calm assurance and abundant joy in the midst of trials and chaos.

But how do we live out this higher life? The key is obtaining childlike trust and faith in God, knowing that through thick and thin, He is with us and *wants* to carry our burdens.

*Thank You, Daddy God, for being
with me through thick and thin.*

Father Knows Best

You are God's child, and God will
give you the blessing he promised,
because you are his child.

Most of us hesitate to give God our burdens because we're not sure He can handle them. It's as though we're telling God that we know better. It's as if *He* is the child and *we* are the father, always knowing what's best. That is a ludicrously fantastic role reversal when the fact of the matter is that *we* are the children and *God* is the Father—the Father who *always* knows best.

··

Remind me, Lord,
that You always know best.

Jesus Does All Things Well

If you are tired from carrying heavy burdens,
come to me and I will give you rest.
MATTHEW 11:28 CEV

How ridiculous for us to think that Jesus—who stilled the wind and waves, healed the deaf, mute, blind, and lame, and rose from the dead—is unable to handle our problems. We must train our minds and hearts to believe what the blind hymn writer Fanny Crosby understood: "For I know that whate'er befall me, Jesus doeth all things well"! Notice her use of the present tense—"doeth." He is with you now, waiting to carry your load. To turn your trial into triumph! Will you let Him?

Lord, please take my burdens as I rest in You.

God's Panoramic Vision

The eyes of the LORD are in every place,
keeping watch on the evil and the good.

PROVERBS 15:3 NKJV

Perhaps we think our prayers are going nowhere. . . that God—too busy with bigger world problems— will not respond. This is a very small view of a God whose eyes are everywhere. With His panoramic vision, He can see the solutions we cannot even begin to imagine. Not only that, but as soon as we cry out to Him, He hears us and responds with His all-encompassing love and affection.

I cry to You, Lord. See me here!
Attend to my prayer!

First Responder

*"Can a mother forget the infant at her breast,
walk away from the baby she bore? But even if
mothers forget, I'd never forget you—never."*

ISAIAH 49:15 MSG

Just as women immediately respond to their infants' cries, God immediately responds to our cries for help. He is always listening, waiting for us to share and let go of all our burdens—the greatest of which is self. We are so often focused on our feelings, our unique temperaments, our own bad habits and temptations, our expectations, fears, and plans that we cannot see clearly. We allow these things to take over our thoughts, to hold us in bondage. But our selves must be abandoned to God.

*Thank You, Lord, for always
keeping me in Your mind and heart.*

Focus

You will keep in perfect peace all who trust in you,
all whose thoughts are fixed on you!
ISAIAH 26:3 NLT

We are to give God all our other burdens—of health, Christian service, careers, husbands, children, households, friends—everything that produces those horrible worry lines. We are often so consumed with the worries of this world that we lose our focus on God. In this information age, we hear bad news from every corner of the world! It's enough to stoop our shoulders. But God reminds us that we are not to carry these burdens. We were not made for it. And when all we can focus on is trouble, we miss God's miracles!

Take all my burdens, Lord,
and leave me Your peace.

Raise More Praise

I will bless the LORD at all times;
His praise shall continually be in my mouth.
PSALM 34:1 NKJV

We need to take a step back, close our mouths, and watch for God working. When we see where and how He is moving, we will be driven to praise instead of petitions!

In June 2012 in Ohio, high school track champion Meghan Vogel saw that a fellow runner had collapsed during the 3,200-meter race. Not only did she pick the girl up and help her finish the race, but she pushed her across the finish line ahead of herself. That is where God is working! This is cause for praise!

Help me, Lord, to raise more
praise than petitions!

Go to God

"Don't worry. Just have faith!"
MARK 5:36 CEV

Our vision is limited. We cannot see the future and are at times uncertain of the present. If we're not focused on or looking for God's working, our imaginations can run away with us. Soon we're thinking of the worst-case scenario, reasoning that we should, after all, be prepared just in case. Before we know it, our thoughts careen out of control. Next our emotions respond, and we sink in despair over an imagined outcome that may never be realized! If only we had begun a heart-to-heart conversation with the heavenly Father before our thoughts could get carried away. Go to God with your troubles and leave them at His feet.

Lord, I need relief! Please take these burdens. . . .

Everything You Need

*Daughter, thy faith hath made
thee whole; go in peace.*

MARK 5:34 KJV

Remember your years as a small child? You didn't worry about your dinner. You knew that in some way when your playtime was over, a meal would be awaiting you. You trusted those who cared for you—your parents, teachers, and at times even those not worthy of your trust. As a child, you provided nothing for yourself; yet whatever you needed, you received. You didn't worry about tomorrow but lived in the now.

Now you are grown, but God still considers you a child. You are His daughter, and He will lovingly provide everything you need—*in the moment!*

*Thank You, good Lord,
for continuing to take care of me.*

Your Security Blanket

*Do not let your hearts be troubled, neither let
them be afraid. [Stop allowing yourselves to
be agitated and disturbed; and do not permit
yourselves to be fearful and intimidated
and cowardly and unsettled.]*

JOHN 14:27 AMPC

Make Jesus your security blanket. Whatever your
issue—yourself, your plans, your husband, your children, your work, the world's woes, your misgivings,
apprehensions, or anxiety—take it to your Lord.
Reach out for His garment. By faith, allow Him to
take your burden away and leave you whole.

Be calm. Be carefree. Become an assured daughter of God, trusting that He will never leave you.
He will never forget you. He has "written your name
on the palms" of His hands (Isaiah 49:16 NIrV).

....

Lord, hold me close and calm my heart.

Living Carefree!

Be careful for nothing.
PHILIPPIANS 4:6 KJV

Let go of the past, present, and future. God has promised to take care of you. It's not a theory, but fact! Look to the lilies and the birds. If God is taking care of them, He is more than attentive to what those created in His image need, want, desire, and deal with, every moment of every day.

Like a nursing mother, when God hears your every sigh, whine, and cry, He responds immediately. You are His precious baby girl. Trust Him as you trust the earth to support you. You are in His hands, hearts, and thoughts. It is in Christ Jesus—who does all things well—that you will find your peace and rest.

Help me, Lord, to live "careful for nothing."

Entering In

*[God] did not spare his own Son but
gave him for us all. So with Jesus,
God will surely give us all things.*

ROMANS 8:32 NCV

Now that we know what the true Christian life is,
how do we enter in? How do we spend our days
confidently cool in the midst of worldly turmoil?

The true Christian experience is not something
we can achieve by any sort of directed effort on our
part. Rather, it is something we gain possession of
by receiving it, as we would a gift from a loved one.

A child does not earn affection from its mother.
Instead, it receives something the mother can't help
but give. So does our Father God give us this life,
as a gift He can't help but express to us.

....

Thank You, Father God, for this life I live in You.

Entirely In

The Lord is good, a Strength and Stronghold
in the day of trouble; He knows (recognizes,
has knowledge of, and understands) those
who take refuge and trust in Him.

NAHUM 1:7 AMPC

Suppose you were a patient who begged a doctor to cure you of a dreaded disease. For that cure to work, you must absolutely obey your doctor or remain disease stricken. That's the same way you must consecrate or commit your life to God. You must put yourself entirely in His hands and allow Him to have His way with you—no matter how you feel or what you judge to be right! This will inevitably lead to a life of blessings and peace in Christ, for God the Father only wants what is best for you.

I commit my soul and self
to You, Lord. I'm in!

God's Immense Love

We love Him, because
He first loved us.
1 JOHN 4:19 AMPC

God Himself is so much more loving to us than we could ever be to one cherished individual. Isn't He the One who gave us His one and only Son to save us from our sins? To save us from ourselves? In fact, He is just aching for us to enter not only the kingdom of God but the kingdom of heaven. Bill Gillham, author of *What God Wishes Christians Knew about Christianity*, wrote, "Christ's death saved you from hell *below* the earth; Christ's life saves you from hell *upon* the earth."

Thank You, Lord,
for loving me so!

Infinite Bliss

*[God] picked us up and set us down in
highest heaven in company with Jesus.*
EPHESIANS 2:6 MSG

In the words of Hannah Whitall Smith:

*Heaven is a place of infinite bliss because His
will is perfectly done there, and our lives share
in this bliss just in proportion as His will is
perfectly done in them. He loves us—loves us,
I say—and the will of love is always blessings
for its loved one. Could we but for one moment
get a glimpse into the mighty depths of His
love, and our hearts would spring out to meet
His will and embrace it as our richest treasure;
and we would abandon ourselves to it with an
enthusiasm of gratitude and joy that such a
wondrous privilege could be ours.*

*Lord, in this place of infinite bliss,
my heart springs to meet Yours.*

From "Then" into "Now"

At one time you refused to obey God.
But now you have received mercy.
ROMANS 11:30–31 NCV

Remember how much Christ loves us and how we cannot be separated from that love? Remember how much He has forgiven us? Unless we believe in this love and forgiveness and claim both as our own, they are not really ours. Yet when it comes to living our lives for Christ, we lose sight of these principles and think that once we're saved and forgiven, we need to live by works and effort. Instead of *receiving* all that He has to offer, we begin to *do*, trying to work our way into the kingdom when in actuality, we have already arrived!

It's a matter of moving from "then" into "now."

I claim Your love and forgiveness,
Lord, as my very own. Amen.

A Present and Now Faith

*He touched their eyes, saying, "It shall
be done to you according to your faith."*

MATTHEW 9:29 NASB

Our words to our loving God must be "Thy will
be done." And in order to say that, we must have
faith—an essential element necessary to receive any
gift. Nothing—especially that which is purely mental or spiritual—ever really becomes ours until we
believe it has been given wholeheartedly and then
claim it as our own precious gift.

Sisters in Christ, how we will live in Christ is
"according to our faith." That has always been the
limit and the rule. And this faith must be a present
and *now* faith.

*Dear Lord, help me make my faith
a present faith, a now faith.*

Jesus Saves

"She will bear a Son; and you shall call His name Jesus, for He will save His people from their sins."
MATTHEW 1:21 NASB

Hannah Whitall Smith wrote, "No faith that looks for a future deliverance from the power of sin will ever lead a soul into the life we are describing. Perhaps no four words in the language have more meaning in them than the following." Repeat the following words over and over again—with your voice, heart, soul, and spirit:

Jesus saves me now. (It is *He* who continually saves you.)

Jesus *saves* me now. (It is His *work*, not yours, *to save you continually*.)

Jesus saves *me* now. (*You are the one* He is continually saving.)

Jesus saves me *now*. (He is saving you *every moment of every day*—right now!)

Dear Lord Jesus, thank You
for saving me over and over again!

Led by the Good Shepherd

The Lord is my shepherd.
I am never in need.

PSALM 23:1 GW

Hidden in Christ, we are led through Psalm 23. We arrive, protected and guided by our Good Shepherd. We are fed in green pastures. Immersed in still, calm waters. We need not fear anything but simply lie down in His luscious field, our souls restored as God originally planned in the Garden of Eden. What a life of rest and triumph in Christ!

The more time we spend in Christ, the more we become like Him and the closer we grow to God. It's a win-win-win!

My rest and life I find in
You alone, Lord.

The Mighty Rock

I will be with thee: I will not fail thee, nor forsake thee. Be strong and of a good courage.

JOSHUA 1:5-6 KJV

John Greenleaf Whittier wrote, "The steps of faith fall on the seeming void, but find the rock beneath." Christ is a mighty Rock on which we stand in this life and for all eternity. So don't be afraid to take steps of faith. With Him as our sure foundation, we will not sink in the sand but stand triumphant upon our Lord and Master.

God will be with us and never leave us. With Him in our corner, His courage and strength in our hearts, and ourselves hidden in Christ, we have assurance that we can indeed cross that river and make it into the Promised Land.

....

*With You, Lord, I find my strength
and courage to walk in faith.*

A God-Shaped Life

*Doing whatever you feel like whenever
you feel like it, and grabbing whatever
attracts your fancy. That's a life shaped
by things and feelings instead of by God.*

COLOSSIANS 3:5 MSG

Just as our soul awakens and begins its upward journey of a higher life in Christ, our feelings challenge that truth. When we base the truth of God and our commitment on what we feel—or don't feel—we're misdirected, thinking perhaps we've not given ourselves over to God at all.

Since our feelings belie the truth, we cannot believe God has us in His hands. "As usual, we put feeling first and faith second, and fact last of all," wrote Hannah Whitall Smith. "Now, God's invariable rule in everything is, fact first, faith second, and feelings last of all."

Lord, shape my life with Your truth. Amen.

Fact, Faith, Then Feelings

She thought, "If I just touch
His garments, I will get well."
MARK 5:28 NASB

This rule of God—fact, faith, then feelings—is confirmed by the woman who'd been hemorrhaging for twelve years. She'd been to numerous doctors, but her condition had only grown worse. Then she heard about Jesus and took His miracle works as *fact*. Instead of allowing feelings of discouragement and hopelessness to override that fact, she resolutely sought Him out amid the crowd. She came from behind Him and touched His robe, thinking, "If I just touch His garments, I will get well." Her *facts* about the situation were followed by her *faith*! The result? She was immediately healed of her malady!

Help me remember to put facts first,
faith second, and feelings last, Lord!

Aligned in God's Order

*Daughter, your faith (your trust and
confidence in Me, springing from faith in
God) has restored you to health. Go in (into)
peace and be continually healed and freed
from your [distressing bodily] disease.*

MARK 5:34 AMPC

What a woman of daring, to make her way through
a crowd and reach out for the Lord's healing power!
And then to admit that she'd done so surely re-
quired even more courage! Her reward? Not only
healing, but having Jesus look and speak directly
to her: "Daughter, your faith has made you well; go
in peace" (Mark 5:34 NASB).

The way to meet the challenge of consecra-
tion, to give yourself entirely to God, is to get in
line with God's order of things—fact, faith, and only
then, feelings.

I give myself entirely to You, Lord.

The Next Step

*In all your ways know, recognize, and
acknowledge Him, and He will direct
and make straight and plain your paths.*

PROVERBS 3:6 AMPC

Are you afraid to turn yourself over completely to God's will? Afraid of losing your personality, which you may have grown fond of over the years? You need not be!

In C. S. Lewis's delightful book *The Screwtape Letters*, a senior devil writes to his minion, "When He [Jesus, their 'Enemy'] talks of their losing their selves, He means only abandoning the clamour of self-will; once they have done that, He really gives them back all their personality, and boasts (I am afraid, sincerely) that when they are wholly His they will be more themselves than ever."

So be courageous. Take the step. Turn yourself over to God.

---

*Make me wholly Yours, Lord, so that
I can be more myself than ever!*

A Settled Thing

*The grace (blessing and favor) of the Lord
Jesus Christ (the Messiah) be with all the
saints (God's holy people, those set apart
for God, to be, as it were, exclusively His).*

REVELATION 22:21 AMPC

Consider it a fact that God has accepted you. Allow
your faith to kick in. Know that you're in His hands,
that He'll work through You to do His will. As the
days go by, don't give in to the idea that nothing
has really changed after all just because you don't
feel it. This kind of wrestling will go on and on unless you cut it short by faith. Hannah Whitall Smith
wrote, "Come to the point of considering that matter an accomplished and settled thing, and leave it
there before you can possibly expect any change of
feeling whatever."

*Thank You, Lord, for accepting me—
lock, stock, and barrel!*

Offer Accepted!

Give your bodies to God because of all he has
done for you. Let them be a living and holy
sacrifice—the kind he will find acceptable.
This is truly the way to worship him.

ROMANS 12:1 NLT

Under Levitical law, everything given to God, because it had been *given*, became something holy, or consecrated (see Leviticus 27:28). It had been set apart. And although we are no longer under Levitical law, there is a parallel. For Romans 12:1 calls us as Christians to give our bodies to God as a living sacrifice. So, having given ourselves to Christ, whose one sacrifice perfected us, we're acceptable to God (see 1 Corinthians 1:30); we're *holy*—whether we feel like it or not!

....

Here I am, Lord. All I am and will
be is Yours for the taking.

Put Right

*In Christ we are put right with God, and have been
made holy, and have been set free from sin.*

1 CORINTHIANS 1:30 NCV

Your thoughts fuel your feelings, and your feelings,
your actions. So if you don't feel consecrated to
God, you certainly won't act like it. This will force
you to try to *act* holy on the surface, trying in your
own power to do all the things a saint should do:
attend church, read the Bible, pray unceasingly,
love others, evangelize, and so forth. In the process, you're wearing yourself out, doing things you
don't feel like doing. Or worse yet, doing nothing
and feeling guilty about it. That's when you need to
remember this: you're a saint not because of what
you've done but because of what *God* has done
for you.

Thank You, Lord, for making me a saint.

Set Apart

You were consecrated (set apart, hallowed),
and you were justified [pronounced righteous,
by trusting] in the name of the Lord Jesus
Christ and in the [Holy] Spirit of our God.

1 CORINTHIANS 6:11 AMPC

Because God has done it all and made you holy, His work is what is going to change your behavior. His power is going to change your life. Since God has already done it, why are you wearing yourself out trying to live right? And why, if you are misbehaving, are you acting as if He hasn't done anything at all?

God has given us all we need to be everything He wants us to be. It is up to us to use what He has given us to make us holy.

Dear Lord, may Your power change my life.

A New Woman

*You've become a new person. This new
person is continually renewed in
knowledge to be like its Creator.*
COLOSSIANS 3:10 GW

God has made you a new woman in Christ! You
have been designed to be what He wants you to be!
And through the power of the Holy Spirit, God has
given you the same power and the same strength as
Christ, to be that new woman.

Being a saint, being *consecrated*, isn't based on
our feelings or our behavior. It's based on the power
God has given us as we have fully committed ourselves to Him. He will work through us, to help us
walk as Christ did, if we just believe. For that we
need faith and prayer.

*Lord, help me, Your "new woman,"
walk as Jesus did.*

Committing Yourself to God

Now faith is the assurance of things hoped for,
the conviction of things not seen.

HEBREWS 11:1 NASB

To make our prayers more effective, we need to believe that God is real—even though He is not visible to our human eyes. We must believe the *fact* that His presence is a certain thing and that He sees everything we do and hears everything we say. This takes the *faith* described in Hebrews 11:1.

If you are not sure you've committed yourself wholeheartedly to God, do so now. Imagine God beside you. Start a heart-to-heart conversation with Him right now. . . .

Dear Lord, in this moment, and for all the moments
to come, I turn myself—mind, body, heart, and soul—
over to You. May Your will be done in my life.

The Remedy

Understand the incredible greatness of God's power for us who believe him. This is the same mighty power that raised Christ from the dead.

EPHESIANS 1:19-20 NLT

You're now in God's hands, ready to receive and *use* the power and strength to do what He wills you to do, to be who He wants you to be. If you begin to doubt your surrender, your wavering faith will cause both you and your experience to be wave and wind tossed. So take the remedy of repeating over and over:

Lord, I'm Your daughter—heart, mind, body, and soul. I give myself entirely to You. I believe You've accepted me, and I put myself entirely in Your hands. Work through me to be the woman You've called me to be. I trust You now and forevermore.

Trust the One

*Now the God of hope fill you with all joy and
peace in believing, that ye may abound in hope,
through the power of the Holy Ghost.*

ROMANS 15:13 KJV

At our first baby steps in this Christian life, we may
have imagined that faith would be something we
could feel, such as a heart overwhelmed with belief
in God when we've received an answer to prayer or
an unexpected blessing. Or we might have just had
surface faith—the faith that we think we can use to
purchase God's blessings.

Yet most often, faith is something that keeps us
looking to the Lord during times of trial, knowing
that we can trust the One who knows so much better than we do.

*God of hope, fill me with the
joy and peace of faith.*

Faith Defined

Things that are seen don't last forever, but things that are not seen are eternal. That's why we keep our minds on the things that cannot be seen.
2 CORINTHIANS 4:18 CEV

Faith is nothing we can see, touch, taste, hear, or smell. Hannah Whitall Smith wrote:

> [Faith] is simply believing God. You see something and thus know that you have sight; you believe something and thus know that you have faith. For as sight is only seeing, so faith is only believing. If you believe the truth, you are saved; if you believe a lie, you are lost. Your salvation comes, not because your faith saves you, but because it links you to the Savior who saves.

Faith then is simply believing God when He says He has done or will do something, then trusting Him to come through.

I believe in You, Lord!

Awakened by Prayers

Jesus was sleeping at the back of the boat....
The disciples woke him up, shouting, "Teacher,
don't you care that we're going to drown?"

MARK 4:38 NLT

Do you think Jesus is sleeping just when you need Him the most? Do you think He's not watching you, that He won't keep you from perishing, that you cannot awaken Him with your prayers? Does your faith disappear the moment you're in danger?

This Savior of yours is the One who stilled the wind and the waves, who brought dead people back to life, who changed water into wine, and healed the blind, deaf, and mute. He's the One who Himself rose from the dead—just to save us! So don't let your thoughts lead you astray the moment you're in peril!

May my thoughts center on You, Lord!

The Power of Thoughts

For as he thinketh in his heart, so is he.

PROVERBS 23:7 KJV

Our thoughts are very powerful. What we believe within will appear without. Our thoughts can even lead us astray. We must continually look to God's Word, write it upon our hearts, and believe that He will do as He has promised. We must imprint the words of Hebrews 11:1 upon our minds: "Now faith is the assurance (the confirmation, the title deed) of the things [we] hope for, being the proof of things [we] do not see and the conviction of their reality [faith perceiving as real fact what is not revealed to the senses]" (AMPC).

Help me build up my faith
thoughts in You, Lord.

Above All

Now unto him that is able to do exceeding abundantly above all that we ask or think, according to the power that worketh in us.

EPHESIANS 3:20 KJV

Perhaps you think you lack faith because you don't feel the working of the Holy Spirit in your life. If you believe this, you have, in effect, not only made God out to be a liar and called false the "record that God gave of his Son" (1 John 5:10 KJV), but you have also lost any confidence in the Holy Spirit. In this regard, the fault lies in your lack of faith in God and His Word, not in the power of the Holy Spirit. Put your thoughts, then, on the side of faith.

Help me, Lord, to put my thoughts on the side of faith. Amen.

Standing Firm

*Though you have not seen Him, you love
Him, and though you do not see Him now,
but believe in Him, you greatly rejoice with
joy inexpressible and full of glory.*

1 PETER 1:8 NASB

Replace every suggestion of doubt—from within or
without—with a statement of faith until, whether
facing triumph or trial, you stand firm in your faith.
Hannah Whitall Smith wrote:

*Out of your very unbelief, throw yourself un-
reservedly on the Word and promises of God,
and dare to abandon yourself to the keeping
and the saving power of the Lord Jesus. If you
have ever trusted a precious interest in the
hands of an earthly friend, I entreat you, trust
yourself and all your spiritual interest now in
the hands of your heavenly Friend, and never,
never, never allow yourself to doubt again.*

Show me, Lord, how to stand firm in my faith.

Active Energy

"Woman, you have strong faith! What you wanted will be done for you." At that moment her daughter was cured.
MATTHEW 15:28 GW

Replace your doubting with knowing. Be like the Canaanite woman (see Matthew 15:21–28) who substituted fretting and fearing with firm faith. Hannah Whitall Smith wrote:

It is a law of spiritual life that every act of trust makes the next act less difficult, until at length, if these acts are persisted in, trusting becomes, like breathing, the natural unconscious action of the redeemed soul.

Therefore put your will into your believing. Your faith must not be a passive imbecility but an active energy. You may have to believe against every appearance, but no matter.

Hear my prayer, Lord! I believe in You!

Unswerving Trust

*If anyone steadfastly believes in Me, he will
himself be able to do the things that I do;
and he will do even greater things than
these, because I go to the Father.*

JOHN 14:12 AMPC

When panic knocks on your door, answer it with
unswerving trust in the Lord. Speak to it with God's
words of faith. Reach for His calm, for His peace.
Don't allow fear and the panicked thump of your
heart to drown out the words God is speaking into
your life. Banish discouragement. . .it's a major
roadblock to your union with God.

Stop your frenzied activity. Take a few deep
breaths. Look into God's Word. Allow it to pen-
etrate Your spirit, soul, and mind. Write it upon
your heart. As you build up your faith, peace will
pervade.

Write Your Word upon my heart, Lord.

Mustard-Seed Faith

"If you have faith the size of a mustard seed,
you could say to this mulberry tree, 'Pull
yourself up by the roots, and plant yourself
in the sea!' and it would obey you."

LUKE 17:6 GW

Begin each day with a mustard-seed faith (see Luke 17:6). Determinedly repeat to yourself, "I believe and trust in my Lord and His power." If you are patient and persistent in this, your worries will fade, your fears will wane, your faith will blossom, and you will share in the Lord's joy to the glory of God who will say, "O woman, great is thy faith" (Matthew 15:28 KJV).

As Saint Augustine said, "Faith is to believe what you do not yet see; the reward for this faith is to see what you believe."

Lord, I believe and trust in You and Your power.

Living in God's Will

This is the confidence which we have before Him, that, if we ask anything according to His will, He hears us.

1 JOHN 5:14 NASB

Our emotions are as volatile as the stock market. When we are riding high, our life of faith seems real. But when we are at our lowest point, we feel we may not have surrendered ourselves to God's will at all. At this juncture, it's important to fall back upon the truth that the life in Christ is not lived in the emotions but in the will. And if we keep our wills consistently abiding in their center—which is God's will, the true reality—our emotional ups and downs will not disturb us.

Help me, Lord, to leave my emotions behind and look to Your will. Amen.

Walking in God's Will

*God. . .is the One who makes everything
agree with what he decides and wants.*
EPHESIANS 1:11 NCV

When we're not walking in God's will, there's dissonance. Only when our will is tied to His, and His will obeyed, will harmony reign within us. That's when the Holy Spirit begins to guide us into right living.

Our emotions are not our true selves. And if God is to take hold of us, it must be into this central will or personality that He enters in. Then if He's reigning within that central will by the power of His Spirit, all the rest of that personality must come under His influence. And as the will is, so is the woman.

*Reign within me, Lord, so that
I may walk in Your will.*

Shifting Your Will

*God is working in you, giving you the desire
and the power to do what pleases him.*
PHILIPPIANS 2:13 NLT

You must shift your will to the believing side. For when you choose to *believe*, you need not worry about how you *feel*. Your emotions will eventually be compelled to come into the harmony of the real you, the woman hidden in Christ, in the secret place of the Father!

At times, you may find great difficulty in controlling your emotions. But you *can* control your will. So you may say firmly and continually, "I give my will to God." Deep inside, you know He *always* knows best.

---

*I choose to give my will to You, Lord,
for You always know best!*

Captive Thoughts

*We use our powerful God-tools for smashing
warped philosophies, tearing down barriers
erected against the truth of God, fitting every
loose thought and emotion and impulse into
the structure of life shaped by Christ.*

2 CORINTHIANS 10:5 MSG

Hannah Whitall Smith wrote: "The real thing in your experience is what your will decides, not your emotions. You are far more in danger of hypocrisy and untruth in yielding to the assertions of your feelings than in holding fast to the decision of your will."

Are your emotions leading you astray? Are your thoughts convincing you that you are a hypocrite, making you feel ashamed? If so, stop. Take a deep breath and rein in your feelings. Then take those thoughts of hypocrisy away, captive to the obedience of Christ.

*Lord, take my thoughts captive and
make them obedient to Jesus Christ.*

Your Hiding Place

*"I will instruct you. I will teach you the
way that you should go. I will advise
you as my eyes watch over you."*

PSALM 32:8 GW

Our powerful emotions are strongholds that can be
pulled down by the truth of the Gospel through the
power, grace, mercy, and love of God.

When we say to the Lord, "You are my hiding
place. You protect me from trouble. You surround
me with joyous songs of salvation" (Psalm 32:7 GW),
He says He'll teach us the way to go. And if we
don't cling stubbornly to our own will, we'll be surrounded by mercy and "be glad and find joy in the
LORD" (Psalm 32:11 GW).

*Lord, teach me Your will and
the way I should go.*

Ask, Seek, Knock

"Ask, and it will be given to you; seek, and you will find; knock, and it will be opened to you. For everyone who asks, receives; and he who seeks, finds; and to him who knocks, it will be opened."

LUKE 11:9–10 NASB

Our joy will be found when we remain in God's will. But how do we find God's will for our lives? By continually coming to Him in prayer, by consistently immersing ourselves in His Word, by constantly seeking Him first!

God does not ask us to seek His will and then go our own way. It's a constant, consistent practice on our part. We're to continue asking, seeking, and knocking. In doing so, we will continue to receive God in our hearts and find His will for our lives. He'll keep on opening doors that have been shut!

I come, Lord, seeking Your will.

God's Kingdom First

*"Don't be concerned about what to eat and what
to drink. Don't worry about such things. These
things dominate the thoughts of unbelievers all
over the world, but your Father already knows
your needs. Seek the Kingdom of God above all
else, and he will give you everything you need."*

LUKE 12:29–31 NLT

You may wonder, *If I follow God's will, how will my
family, my friends, my loved ones fare?*

Not to worry. All you need to do is seek God's
kingdom first; everything else will fall in line! When
you live in God's will and are hidden in Christ, you
take up residence in the worry-free zone, a place
where emotions amount to naught, where they become mere specks of dust floating on the surface of
your mind.

It is You and Your kingdom I seek first, Lord.

Back to the Beginning

"This is the promise that I will make to them after those days, says the Lord: 'I will put my teachings in their hearts and write them in their minds.'"

HEBREWS 10:16 GW

We cannot wrestle with God's will for our lives. If we do, we will end up limping around like Jacob. But when our wills work with God's, we are indeed powers to be reckoned with! And this is amazing because it is what we were created to do from the very beginning. Before the Fall, our natural state was in total harmony with God. We're just getting right back to the beginning!

Please, Lord, help my will to work with and be attuned to Yours.

Your Real Master

*We ask this so that you will live the kind of
lives that prove you belong to the Lord. Then
you will want to please him in every way as
you grow in producing every kind of good
work by this knowledge about God.*

COLOSSIANS 1:10 GW

In the midst of our daily activities, we do not need
to know or understand all God is doing. We merely
need to take a step back and focus on Jesus. We
don't need to fear God's will but trust Him, resting
in the truth that He knows what He's doing.

So consider your emotions as nothing more
than servants and regard your will in God's as the
real master of your being. When you do, you'll find
that you can ignore your emotions and instead
focus on the state of your will.

*Help me, Lord, to focus on You,
not my emotions.*

Trusting God

God, see what is in my heart. Know what is there.
Test me. Know what I'm thinking. See if there's
anything in my life you don't like. Help me
live in the way that is always right.
PSALM 139:23-24 NIrV

In following God's will for your life, you may not always see the picture or the outcome He has in mind. But that's okay. All you need to do is trust God and present yourself to Him as a living sacrifice. Trust Him to move in your life. Hannah Whitall Smith tells us to remember that we're not giving up our wills but are simply substituting the "higher, divine, mature will of God for our foolish, misdirected wills of ignorance and immaturity."

In this moment, Lord,
substitute my will for Yours.

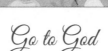

Go to God

*If any of you is deficient in wisdom, let him
ask of the giving God [Who gives] to everyone
liberally and ungrudgingly, without reproaching
or faultfinding, and it will be given him.*

JAMES 1:5 AMPC

You are on the initial steps of the pathway to a life of faith. You have given yourself to God—mind, body, soul, and spirit. You are in His hands, and He is shaping you into a new creature with a divine purpose. You have determined to keep your will in agreement with His. You are, in effect, trusting Him with everything. But now you may be unsure of the next step. You know God has a purpose for your life, but which direction should you go? Just go to God and ask Him.

Lord, I need Your wisdom.
What's our next step?

The Right Path

The Comforter (Counselor, Helper, Intercessor,
Advocate, Strengthener, Standby), the Holy
Spirit, Whom the Father will send in My name
[in My place, to represent Me and act on My
behalf], He will teach you all things. And He will
cause you to recall (will remind you of, bring to
your remembrance) everything I have told you.

JOHN 14:26 AMPC

Be certain of two things: the first is that you really
and truly do intend to obey the Lord in all things.
And if this is so, you must understand that the
Father, Son, and Holy Spirit are determined to
make their will known to you and to guide you
down the right path—every step of the way. In fact,
they have promised to do so!

Father, Son, Spirit, teach me, tell me,
guide me down the right path.

No Doubt

*Only it must be in faith that he asks with
no wavering (no hesitating, no doubting).
For the one who wavers (hesitates, doubts) is
like the billowing surge out at sea that is blown
hither and thither and tossed by the wind.*

JAMES 1:6 AMPC

With the Father, Son, and Holy Spirit on your side, you cannot get lost. You never need to fear anything! If you confidently believe in God the Father, His Son Jesus, and the Holy Spirit, and if you determine to look for and expect their guidance, you will receive it. But you must not doubt.

God will give you guidance if you seek it in faith, with confidence that He will give it. In addition, you must keep in mind that God knows absolutely everything!

---

*I seek Your face and guidance, Lord.
For You know all. In Your name I pray, amen.*

The Entire Picture

"Anyone who comes to me but refuses to let go of father, mother, spouse, children, brothers, sisters— yes, even one's own self!—can't be my disciple."

LUKE 14:26 MSG

Regardless of how you or those around you see confusion and loss in the path God has chosen for you, He knows exactly what blessings await. Although you may not understand His road map for you, remember that with your human vision, you see only a portion of the map. But God sees the entire picture, and His vision can be trusted.

Jesus has told us to let go of all but God. In doing so, we may discover that to follow Jesus, we are called to forsake, inwardly, everyone in our lives— including ourselves!

*I let go of all and trust
in Your vision, Lord.*

In Sync

For You are my rock and my fortress; for Your name's sake You will lead me and guide me.

PSALM 31:3 NASB

We may be guided to paths that those we love most will disapprove of. For this we must be prepared. We must continually tell ourselves that God is in control. He knows all—including what's best for us.

But how does God give us His guidance? In four simple ways: through His Word, through providential circumstances, through our spiritually enlightened judgment, and through the inward promptings of the Holy Spirit upon our minds. When these four harmonize, when they are all in sync, we know God's hand is guiding us.

....

Guide me, Lord, today—in every way.

Through His Word

Every Scripture passage is inspired by God.
All of them are useful for teaching, pointing
out errors, correcting people, and training
them for a life that has God's approval.

2 TIMOTHY 3:16 GW

If your road map bypasses scripture, beware: you are headed for a dead end. If you are confused about which path to take, you are directed to consult God's Word (see 2 Timothy 3:16–17). If the Bible provides guidance in that particular regard, ask the Holy Spirit to make everything clear to you. Then obey. But be careful not to take scripture out of context, just because that's the answer or the guidance you endeavor to have.

As I open God's Word, Holy Spirit,
make the truth clear to me.

Waiting on Wisdom

Wait and hope for and expect the Lord;
be brave and of good courage and let
your heart be stout and enduring.

PSALM 27:14 AMPC

Hannah Whitall Smith wrote: "The Bible is a book of principles and not a book of disjointed aphorisms. Isolated texts can be made to give approval to things which the principles of scripture are totally opposed." So, be careful not to read what You *want* to see in God's Word. And if you cannot find a clear answer in the Bible, seek guidance through circumstances, your intelligence, and the Spirit's prompting. If any of these tests fails, you need to stop. Wait on the Lord. Watch for Him to move. Eventually, He'll give you the wisdom you seek.

I wait on You, Lord, for the wisdom I seek. Amen.

Through Providential Circumstances

*May He grant you according to your
heart's desire and fulfill all your plans.*

PSALM 20:4 AMPC

One of the ways God gives you guidance is through providential circumstances. Take a look at what's happening in your life. Perhaps you've been content in a career, only to find yourself laid off. You thought the road was clear but now find yourself stranded, not knowing which way to turn. Sometimes losing a job can be the best thing that ever happened to you! For now, you have an opportunity to do that thing you've wanted to do for a long time. God has, in effect, pushed you out of your comfort zone so that you'll be moved to do what He's clearly called you to do!

*Lord, through the events happening in my life,
please make clear what You'd have me do.*

That Familiar Voice

*"When he brings out his own sheep,
he goes before them; and the sheep
follow him, for they know his voice."*

JOHN 10:4 NKJV

If our circumstances are truly providential, God will open doors for us—we won't have to break them down. In other words, if our direction is truly from God, He will go before us and pave the way. Mary Slessor of Calabar wrote, "If I have done anything in my life, it has been easy because the Master has gone before." This is confirmed by Jesus' words in John 10:4 (see above).

Thank You, Lord, for clearing the path before me, paving the way to where You'd have me go and what You'd have me do. Amen.

Through Spiritually Enlightened Judgment

The Lord says, "I will instruct you. I will teach you the way that you should go. I will advise you as my eyes watch over you."

Psalm 32:8 GW

God wants us to use our God-given gifts and intelligence to find our pathway. Although we are not to depend on our own reasoning or common sense, we can use spiritually enlightened judgment to find our way. God will speak to us through the abilities He has given us. In other words, if we have two left feet, He will not call upon us to be ballet dancers. If we are tone deaf, He won't call us to be on the worship team.

Speak, Lord, through the gifts You've given me. Where would You have me use them?

Through the Holy Spirit's Promptings

*The Holy Spirit kept them from speaking
the word in the province of Asia.*

ACTS 16:6 GW

God's guidance can be discovered through following the cues given by the Holy Spirit. If you sense the Spirit putting up roadblocks, prompting you to stop dead in your tracks—*stop!* Wait until all barriers are removed before forging ahead.

But if your barrier is merely fear, if you are uncomfortable about a new endeavor or direction, that may not be the Holy Spirit saying, "Stop." It may simply mean that God is going to stretch you spiritually and mentally or is about to pull you back from a path on which you may have strayed.

*Speak to me, Spirit. My ears
are open, ready to hear.*

God's Guiding Voice

Trust GOD from the bottom of your heart.... Listen
for GOD's voice in everything you do, everywhere
you go; he's the one who will keep you on track.
PROVERBS 3:5–6 MSG

Be aware that anything that provokes dissonance
of the divine harmony within you must be rejected
as not coming from God but from other sources.
The strong personalities in our lives influence us
greatly. So do our temporal circumstances and con-
ditions, which sway us more than we know. In these
instances, your worldly desire to want a particular
thing may threaten to override God's guiding voice.
But you must not let it. Instead, do all You can to
tune into God's familiar voice.

....

Help me, Lord, to stay tuned to
Your guiding voice and no other.

Your GPS

Your ears shall hear a word behind you, saying,
"This is the way, walk in it," whenever you turn to
the right hand or whenever you turn to the left.

ISAIAH 30:21 NKJV

Your spiritual enemy may try to provoke dissonance within You. Remember Eve in the garden? She listened to the wrong voice, which led to her—and the world's—fall. It's not enough to feel you're being led to a new endeavor or action. You must discern the source of the voice calling you before you rush off down the path. Step back. Take the time to find the true voice—no matter how long you may have to wait. Listen carefully. Then, when you hear the Spirit speak, allow Him to be your GPS (God's positioning system).

Speak, Spirit of God. I'm listening.

God's Good Plans

"For I know the plans I have for you," says the
LORD. "They are plans for good and not for
disaster, to give you a future and a hope."
JEREMIAH 29:11 NLT

Endeavor to discern God's guidance by using, along with these four tests—through God's Word, providential circumstances, our spiritually enlightened judgment, and the inward promptings of the Holy Spirit upon our minds—what Hannah Whitall Smith calls "a divine sense of 'oughtness' derived from the harmony of all God's voices." When you do, you will have nothing to fear. If you have faith in Him, if you trust Him with everything, you will have the courage and strength to walk the way He's leading, your hand in His.

Thank You, Lord, for leading me, showing me
Your way in accordance with Your plan.

Soul Rest

*Stand by the roads and look; and ask for the
eternal paths, where the good, old way is; then
walk in it, and you will find rest for your souls.*
JEREMIAH 6:16 AMPC

Know that God will lead you, give you the courage
you need to embark upon every new path, and be
with You every step of the way.

Remember, there is no fear for those living this
higher life if they live each moment of every day
under God's guidance. It is the most wonderful
privilege and promise that we have been given and
leads to a myriad of rewards.

"Rejoice in it. Embrace it eagerly," Hannah
Whitall Smith wrote. "Let everything go that it may
be yours."

*Lord, walking with You along Your good
old way makes me content. For on Your
pathway, I find rest for my soul.*

Lavish Love

*The faithful love of the LORD never ends! His
mercies never cease. Great is his faithfulness;
his mercies begin afresh each morning.*

LAMENTATIONS 3:22–23 NLT

If you have entertained doubts about your sins being forgiven or your unworthiness before God, be assured: God came to save you. In fact, He told you that He "came not to call the righteous, but sinners to repentance" (Luke 5:32 KJV). Hannah Whitall Smith wrote, "Your very sinfulness and unworthiness, instead of being a reason why He should not love you and care for you, are really your chief claim upon His love and His care"! What a wonderful truth to meditate on. He truly does care for and love us, and shame on us for doubting such lavish care and love.

*My faithful Lord of light, thank You
for loving and saving me. Amen.*

God's Embrace

*His father saw him and was moved with pity
and tenderness [for him]; and he ran and
embraced him and kissed him [fervently].*

LUKE 15:20 AMPC

Remember the tale of the prodigal son and the joy
of the father upon his son's return? If not, reread
Luke 15:11–32. We are not perfect; yet, in spite of our
faults, while we are still a long way off, our Father
God sees us and is "moved with pity and tenderness" for us. He runs to us, embraces us, and kisses
us "fervently." Then He celebrates our return! This
happens each time we stray.

*Thank You, Lord, for willingly loving me with
such tenderness, compassion, and fervor.*

Unfailing Love and Comfort

*I cried out, "I am slipping!" but your unfailing love,
O LORD, supported me. When doubts filled my mind,
your comfort gave me renewed hope and cheer.*

PSALM 94:18–19 NLT

Perhaps you feel unworthy of receiving God's promises. Perhaps temptations have gotten the best of you and you sinned to the point of believing God would be well rid of you.

Any accusations that come into your head about your behavior and mistakes come from one source—the enemy. He brings charges against you, day and night (see Revelation 12:10). And if you listen to—and believe—his case against you, you may find yourself in agreement with him. The only things left then are doubt and discouragement. But there is a way out through God's unfailing love and comfort.

*Thank You, Lord, for lifting me with
Your unfailing love and comfort.*

The Key

The Lord will deliver me from every evil attack and will bring me safely into his heavenly Kingdom.

2 TIMOTHY 4:18 NLT

In *The Pilgrim's Progress*, John Bunyan's classic Christian allegory, the characters Christian and his companion Hope are facing the same dark side of life. Having been beaten and tortured, they are being kept prisoner by Giant Despair in Doubting Castle. When all seems lost, Christian suddenly has an *aha!* moment. He has a key called Promise that will "open any lock in Doubting Castle." With that key of Promise, Christian unlocked the dungeon door's bolt, which easily flew open. Then he used that same key to open an outer door and the iron gate, allowing both prisoners to escape!

....

When doubt or despair threaten to overtake me, Lord, remind me of Your promises.

No More Barriers

"You will have complete and free access to God's kingdom, keys to open any and every door: no more barriers between heaven and earth, earth and heaven."

MATTHEW 16:19 MSG

Ladies, we have keys, just like Bunyan's character Christian! Jesus Christ gave those keys to us! Thus, we have "complete and free access to God's kingdom, keys to open any and every door." So rid yourself of any doubts, which only lead to despair. Sink your teeth into God's promises. He already knows all about you. He's known you and loved you since *before* you were born! And He'll continue to love and take care of you all the way into eternity!

Thank You, Lord, for removing all barriers between us! You are an awesome God!

Look to the Promises

Not a single one of all the good promises the
LORD had given to the family of Israel was left
unfulfilled; everything he had spoken came true.
JOSHUA 21:45 NLT

Perhaps we're embarrassed, even ashamed, to admit to Jesus that we have doubts. So instead of praying about them, we suppress them. On this despairing heap, we add guilt as a sort of cherry on top, making ourselves even more miserable and distancing ourselves further from God. Or perhaps we are afraid, like Sarah, who laughed when God told her she would be a mother.

Look to the promises in God's Word. They are for all of us, and they never fail.

Lord, help me to look to Your good
promises, which never ever fail.

Surrender All Doubts

"God is not like people.... When he says something,
he does it. When he makes a promise, he keeps it."
NUMBERS 23:19 GW

When you live your life outside the promises of God, you're no longer focused on Jesus. You're like Peter, sinking in the sea because you've turned your sight to the wind and water. You've taken your eyes off Jesus.

If you have doubts, surrender them to Jesus. Tell Him, "I do believe; help me overcome my unbelief!" (Mark 9:24 NIV). He'll remind you that not only is nothing impossible for Him, that "no word from God will ever fail" (Luke 1:37 NIV), but also that "everything is possible for one who believes"! (Mark 9:23 NIV).

I believe, Lord! Help me
overcome my unbelief!

The Shield of Faith

My defense and shield depend on God,
Who saves the upright in heart.

PSALM 7:10 AMPC

When doubts begin creeping back in, do not despair. Turn them over to the Lord. Protect yourself with the shield of faith. Arm yourself with "the sword of the Spirit, which is the word of God" (Ephesians 6:17 NIV). By reciting God's promises (mentally or aloud), you will be putting your focus back where it belongs—on Jesus. And although the doubts—arrows of the enemy—may clamor against your shield, they will not be able to hurt you.

Thank You, Lord, for arming and
protecting me, keeping me from harm.

A Morning Prayer

"Don't be afraid! Stand still, and see what the LORD will do to save you today. You will never see these Egyptians again. The LORD is fighting for you! So be still!"

EXODUS 14:13–14 GW

For further defense against doubts and discouragement, say this prayer as soon as you awaken every morning:

Good morning, Lord. You are my Abba Father. I am Your daughter whom You dearly love and have forgiven, every moment of every day—even before I was born. Because Jesus has saved me, I am Yours completely. I remain focused on Him. I stand firm in my faith with God as my divine supplier, Christ as my Rock and Refuge, and the Holy Spirit as my Comforter and guiding light. In this I have peace and joy. Amen.

Temptation

If anyone loves the world, the love of the Father is not in him. For all that is in the world—the lust of the flesh, the lust of the eyes, and the pride of life—is not of the Father but is of the world.

1 JOHN 2:15-16 NKJV, EMPHASIS ADDED

There's a general misconception that once we enter the life of faith, temptations and our yielding to them will cease. Yet the reality is that the evil one will tempt us to look to him, the world, or our flesh to meet our needs. In other words, he'll tempt us to act independently of God. Such temptation approaches us via three channels: the lust of the flesh, the lust of the eyes, and the pride of life. Ask the heavenly Father to help you keep your focus on Him today.

*Help me, Lord, to love
You but not the world.*

The Long Way

God did not lead them by way of the land of the
Philistines, although that was near; for God said,
"Lest perhaps the people change their minds
when they see war, and return to Egypt."

EXODUS 13:17 NKJV

The severity and power of your temptations—no matter what channel Satan has used to reach you—may be the strongest proof that you're in the land of promise you've sought. After all, when the Israelites first left Egypt, God took them the long way around the Philistines. But later, when they had more faith in God, He allowed them to be involved in a few skirmishes while in the wilderness, perhaps to test their mettle. It wasn't until they were entering the Promised Land that the real battles began.

Thank You, Lord, for leading me
to the land of Your promises! Amen.

The Right Direction

*Surely He shall deliver you from the snare
of the fowler.... He shall cover you with His
feathers, and under His wings you shall take
refuge; His truth shall be your shield and
buckler. You shall not be afraid.*
PSALM 91:3–5 NKJV

If you are facing a myriad of temptations, some stronger than others, you can know, oddly enough, that you are headed in the right direction and that God will get you through. He will help you find your way out and around whatever is enticing you. As He does so, what you need to do is to remain confident in God, focused, joyful, firm in faith, patient, prayerful, planted in the Word, and steadfast in Christ.

*Deliver me, Lord. Be my Shield,
Buckler, and Refuge.*

Remain Confident

Let not your heart be troubled,
neither let it be afraid.
JOHN 14:27 KJV

In overcoming temptations, confidence is the first thing, confidence is the second thing, and confidence is the third thing. In other words, we cannot let the fact that we're facing temptation discourage us but stand confident in our faith and its strength instead. When Joshua was about to enter the Promised Land and face many foes, God told him, "Be strong and of a good courage. . . . Be not afraid, neither be thou dismayed. . . . Only be thou strong and very courageous" (Joshua 1:6, 9, 7 KJV). And Jesus reinforces this command in John 14:27.

Lord, help me stand confident
and strong in my faith!

Remain Focused

We must focus on Jesus,
the source and goal of our faith.
HEBREWS 12:2 GW

Do not become discouraged when you face temptations. Instead, turn away from them and look for God to deliver you. Understand that He might not do it when or in the way you expect, for He has told us, "My thoughts are not your thoughts, nor are your ways My ways" (Isaiah 55:8 NKJV). But know and understand that He will do it! Put your confidence on the believing side—God's side, the winning side! He has overcome the world! Keep your eyes on the Champion.

My eyes are on You, Lord. In doing so,
I can turn away from temptation
and look for You to deliver me!

Remain Joyful

*Be not grieved and depressed, for the joy of
the Lord is your strength and stronghold.*

NEHEMIAH 8:10 AMPC

Above all, "count it all joy when you fall into various trials" and temptations (James 1:2 NKJV). Don't be brought low in your attitude, thoughts, and demeanor in the middle of the battle. The joy of the Lord will give you the strength you need in the midst of your weakness. Want to really catch the devil off guard? When temptation whispers in your ear, start worshipping the Lord! The evil one won't know what hit him!

....

*In You, Lord, I find joy! All praise
to You and Your strength!*

Remain Firm in Faith

"You won't fight this battle. Instead, take your position, stand still, and see the victory of the LORD.... Don't be frightened or terrified. Tomorrow go out to face them. The LORD is with you."

2 CHRONICLES 20:17 GW

Keep your faith that God will deliver you from whatever temptations you face. Believe that His promises to fight your battles are true. In fact, "the LORD your God walks in the midst of your camp, to deliver you and give your enemies over to you" (Deuteronomy 23:14 NKJV). But you must stand there with Him, for "the LORD is with you when you are with Him" (2 Chronicles 15:2 NASB). If you suddenly can't find God, *you* are the one who has moved—not Him!

With You, Lord, I'll stand still and see Your victory!

Remain Patient

The testing of your faith produces patience.
But let patience have its perfect work, that you
may be perfect and complete, lacking nothing.

JAMES 1:3–4 NKJV

To remain firm in faith, you must practice patience. Give God time to work. He won't fail, for He says "no weapon that is formed against thee shall prosper" (Isaiah 54:17 KJV). He'll help you find a way out. Don't trust in yourself, for you're not strong enough. You need the power of God's Holy Spirit working *through* you (see Acts 1:8). It's God who will arm you with the strength you need (see Psalm 18:32, 37). So step aside. Let Him take up the battle.

I'm trusting in You, Lord, knowing
You will arm me with Your strength.

Remain Prayerful

*If any of you is deficient in wisdom, let him
ask of the giving God [Who gives] to everyone
liberally and ungrudgingly, without reproaching
or faultfinding, and it will be given him.*

JAMES 1:5 AMPC

As you work with God to remain confident, focused, joyful, firm in faith, and patient, back all of those things up with prayer, perhaps not so much for the removal of the temptation but for the wisdom and the strength to face it and learn from it. Remember, God says: "I know what I'm doing. I have it all planned out—plans to take care of you, not abandon you, plans to give you the future you hope for. When you call on me, when you come and pray to me, I'll listen" (Jeremiah 29:11–12 MSG).

*Lord, as You work out Your plan,
I ask for Your wisdom.*

Remain Planted in the Word

*"It is written, 'Man shall not live on
bread alone, but on every word that
proceeds out of the mouth of God.'"*

MATTHEW 4:4 NASB

Scripture is great soil. We're bound to wither and weaken amid temptation—and in many other ways—if we remove ourselves from God's Word. We'll also be standing somewhere in the dark and without water. Jesus' greatest weapon when tempted in the desert was the Word of God (see Matthew 4:1–11). When you feel yourself being enticed, dig yourself deep in the Word. Memorize verses that will help you build the strongest barbed wire fence of protection to keep the evil one from nibbling at your resolve.

*Lord, plant Your Word and all
its wonders in my heart.*

Remain Steadfast in Christ

Blessed are those who endure when they are tested.
When they pass the test, they will receive the crown
of life that God has promised to those who love him.

JAMES 1:12 GW

Be sure and steady in your intentions to stand firm in Christ (see James 1:6–8) for you can do all things through Christ who strengthens you (see Philippians 4:13). "For the LORD will be your confidence, and will keep your foot from being caught" (Proverbs 3:26 NKJV). So flee from the evil one and run to God. Hide beneath His wings. Do not walk out from underneath His protection by doubting. Stand still. Stand firm. And you will not only escape but will also be blessed.

Lord, because of my love for You,
I stand firm in You!

Choosing Sides

"Choose for yourselves this day whom
you will serve.... As for me and my
house, we will serve the Lord."

JOSHUA 24:15 NKJV

Although we may encounter temptations, if we are wholly in God's camp—mind, body, spirit, and soul—we will abhor them. We must especially guard ourselves from those temptations in which we love to indulge. For as George Eliot wrote, "No evil dooms us hopelessly except the evil we love, and desire to continue in, and make no effort to escape from." So make up your mind, now, today, whose camp you are living in, whose side you are on.

I'm in Your camp, Lord. You are
the One I choose to serve.

Pitching Your Tent

"Because he has set his love upon Me,
therefore I will deliver him.... He shall
call upon Me, and I will answer him."

PSALM 91:14–15 NKJV

If you are looking to the things of this world to save you—chocolate or french fries, a new dress or purse or shoes, riches or fame—or to the worldlings themselves, you have taken your eyes off God. You've strayed from your base camp and entered a vast wilderness. Remember to choose the One who has overcome the world, the One in whom you will have success and prosper in all things! Pull up stakes and pitch your tent on God's side once again!

I'm pitching my tent in Your camp,
Lord! For You're the true King!

Your Source of Confidence

You are my hope; O Lord God, You are my trust
from my youth and the source of my confidence.
PSALM 71:5 AMPC

"We must then commit ourselves to the Lord for victory over our temptations, as we committed ourselves at first for forgiveness," Hannah Whitall Smith wrote. "And we must leave ourselves just as utterly in His hands for one as for the other."

Remember that God is faithful. He's put up an exit sign just for you, and you'll find it if your eyes are open. He will show you a way to escape temptation—even when there seems to be no way (see 1 Corinthians 10:13). You need to keep your eyes, heart, thoughts, spirit, and soul on Him, and your faith *in* Him. He—and He *alone*—is your confidence.

You, Lord, are my hope,
trust, and confidence! Amen.

The Reason and Remedy

*If we confess our sins, He is faithful and
righteous to forgive us our sins and to
cleanse us from all unrighteousness.*

1 JOHN 1:9 NASB

Because we are not perfect, we do sometimes
fall short of the standards God has set for us (see
Romans 3:23)—we miss the mark, or sin. The sin we
are discussing here is intentional sin (conscious,
overt acts in defiance of God) as opposed to un-
intentional (through ignorance, with no malice
aforethought). The only real pathway available us,
then, is to face that fact that we have indeed sinned,
confess it to God, and discover, if possible, the
reason and the remedy. Our divine union with
God requires absolute honesty with Him and with
ourselves.

*Lord, I've missed the mark. Please help me find the
reason and remedy. In Your name I pray, amen.*

God's Way

*Have mercy upon me, O God, according
to Your lovingkindness; according to the
multitude of Your tender mercies, blot out my
transgressions. Wash me thoroughly from
my iniquity, and cleanse me from my sin.*

PSALM 51:1–2 NKJV

When we fail, we really have no cause for discouragement and giving up. We must recognize we're not talking about a *state* but a *walk* of life with Christ. Hannah Whitall Smith wrote, "The highway of holiness is not a *place*, but a *way*." Hidden in Christ, we're followers of the Way. We must be aware of where we are. If we've turned off the path, we must instantly return to the route the Father has mapped out for us, trusting Him more than ever!

*Forgive me, Lord. And help me find my
way back to You and Your Way.*

A Better Idea

*"Get up! Why do you
lie thus on your face?"*
JOSHUA 7:10 NKJV

Chances are you've suffered from despair and discouragement. . .as if you've had the spirit knocked out of you. You become immobilized, not wanting to take another step backward or forward. Your discouragement leaves you in a sort of limbo, a place where there's no growth, no progress, no future. After such an overwhelming failure—emotionally, physically, mentally, spiritually—you may find it easier to wallow in your despondency, your face on the ground and dust on your head, than to look up to God. But God, as always, has a better idea. As He told Joshua, He tells you, *"Get up!"*

*I no longer want to live in the land of
discouragement, Lord. Help me get up!*

God's Faithful Forgiveness

*If we confess our sins, he is faithful
and just to forgive us our sins, and to
cleanse us from all unrighteousness.*

1 JOHN 1:9 KJV

What keeps us from lifting our heads? Perhaps it's the thought God will find it hard to forgive us. In fact, He may not forgive us at all! Or if He does, it may take Him days, perhaps years, to get over it. Thank God our Father is not like that. As soon as we come to Him and confess our sins, He forgives! Immediately! There is no silent treatment, no grudge. *And this we must believe!* For if we don't, we've made God out to be a liar (see 1 John 5:10).

Thank You, Lord, for forgiving me!

Looking to Jesus

*Let us run with patience the race that
is set before us, looking unto Jesus.*

HEBREWS 12:1–2 KJV

As soon as consciousness of our sin has set in, we must immediately lift our faces to God and become conscious of His forgiveness. We can only continue walking on this path of holiness by taking our eyes off our misstep and begin "looking unto Jesus" (Hebrews 12:2 KJV). Otherwise, we will keep tripping up!

Once our eyes are back on Him, we can confess what we have done. Within that confession may lie our motives.

----

*I am looking to You, Jesus. Help
me through this life in You.*

Rise Early

*"Do not be afraid, nor be dismayed; take all the
people of war with you, and arise, go up to Ai.
See, I have given into your hand the king of
Ai, his people, his city, and his land."*

JOSHUA 8:1 NKJV

When we have sinned, we need to acknowledge
it. We must be like the children of Israel in Joshua
7. We must rise "early in the morning" (Joshua 7:16
KJV), run to where the sins are hidden, take them
from the midst of their hiding places, and lay them
before the Lord (see Joshua 7:22–23). Then we can
stone them, burn them, and bury them (see Joshua
7:25–26) and immediately receive God's forgiveness, encouragement, and victory, as did Joshua
and the Israelites.

*I rise early and lay my "hidden" missteps
before You, Lord. Please forgive me.*

Abandoned to God

*As far as the east is from the west, so far
has He removed our transgressions from us.*
PSALM 103:12 NKJV

Hannah Whitall Smith wrote:

> *Our courage must rise higher than ever, and
> we must abandon ourselves more completely
> to the Lord that His mighty power may the
> more perfectly work in us. . . . We must forget
> our sin as soon as it is thus confessed and
> forgiven. We must not dwell on it and exam-
> ine it and indulge in a luxury of distress and
> remorse.*

If we do not do as Smith suggests, we will get deeper
and deeper into our sin and further away from God,
putting a sin barrier between us and Him.

*As my courage rises, I abandon myself
even more to You, Lord of forgiveness.*

Our Continual Plea

For once you were full of darkness, but now you
have light from the Lord. So live as people of light!
EPHESIANS 5:8 NLT

To prevent failures and their inevitable discouragements and consequences or to discover their causes if we find we've erred, we must make the following words our continual plea before God: "Investigate my life, O God, find out everything about me; cross-examine and test me, get a clear picture of what I'm about; see for yourself whether I've done anything wrong—then guide me on the road to eternal life" (Psalm 139:23–24 MSG). If we do so, God will rescue us "from our enemies so we can serve God without fear, in holiness and righteousness for as long as we live" (Luke 1:74–75 NLT).

Lord, help me live in Your light!

See God in Everything

The LORD is on my side; I will not fear.
PSALM 118:6 NKJV

Hannah Whitall Smith wrote:

Things in which we can see God's hands always have a sweetness in them that comforts while it wounds. But the trials inflicted by man are full of nothing but bitterness. What is needed, then, is to see God in everything and to receive everything directly from His hands with no intervention of second causes. And it is to this that we must be brought before we can know an abiding experience of entire abandonment and perfect trust. Our abandonment must be to God, not to man. And our trust must be in Him, not in any arm of flesh, or we shall fail at the first trial.

In You alone I trust, Lord.

Your Father's Hand

"God cares. . . . He pays even greater attention to you, down to the last detail—even numbering the hairs on your head!"

MATTHEW 10:29-30 MSG

Hannah Whitall Smith says there are no "second causes" for the believing Christian—that everything comes to us through our Father's hand and with His knowledge, no matter what person or circumstances may have been the apparent agents. This is backed up by God's Word in regard to falling sparrows and hairs on your head (Matthew 10:29-30 above). You'll find even more support in Romans 12:19, 8:31; Psalm 23:1, 118:6; Isaiah 43:2; Daniel 6:22; and Hebrews 13:5-6.

Second causes are under the management of our Father. Not one of them can reach us without God's permission and knowledge.

Thank You, Lord, for watching over me. Amen.

No Overflow

"When you pass through the waters, I will be with you; and through the rivers, they shall not overflow you. When you walk through the fire, you shall not be burned, nor shall the flame scorch you."

ISAIAH 43:2 NKJV

Everything (except our own sinfulness) comes from our Lord. "It may be the sin of man that originates the action, and therefore the thing itself cannot be said to be the will of God," Hannah Whitall Smith wrote, "but by the time it reaches us, it has become God's will for us and must be accepted as coming directly from His hands."

And never forget that, through it all, God will be with you, laughing with you during times of joy and comforting you through times of trial.

I thank You, Lord, for being with me through times of joy and trial.

The One Who Pauses

A Samaritan. . .came where the man was;
and when he saw him, he took pity on him.
LUKE 10:33 NIV

Imagine you've been beaten and robbed and are lying on the roadside. Others may pass by, but you look up at the One who has paused by your side. It's Jesus. He'll put oil on your wounds, bandage you up, pick you up, and carry you to a place of comfort and provision until you can rise again.

In all things, be patient and totally abandoned to God's will and way—to His plan for you—through every blessing as well as every trial. For God loved Jesus as much on the cross as He did on the mount of transfiguration.

I look to You, Lord. You're the
One who pauses by my side.

From Trial to Blessing

*While Joseph was in prison, the LORD was with
him. The LORD reached out to him with his
unchanging love and gave him protection...
and made whatever he did successful.*

GENESIS 39:20–21, 23 GW

We are like a child in God's arms. Everything that
touches us goes through Him first. We must understand that no evil exists—no matter how dark and
bleak—that God cannot turn into good.

Through all Joseph's trials and successes,
Father God was with him—and Joseph stayed with
God. Because Joseph stayed close to the Lord, our
Creator God turned Joseph's trial into a blessing—
not only for Joseph himself but for the sons of
Israel! And He promises to do the same for us!

I rest like a child in Your arms, Lord.

For the Good

*In all things God works for the good of
those who love him, who have been
called according to his purpose.*

ROMANS 8:28 NIV

God is not the author of sin, but He uses His creativity and His wisdom to work the design of His providence to His—and our—advantage. All we need to do is trust Him to work things out for our good. He will overrule events, trials, and tragedies in our lives to His glory and our praise!

Being women, we often try to fix things, and then we become frustrated when we can't. Those are times when we need to let go and let God. Because *He* is the "Great Fixer."

I praise You, my Lord, the Great Fixer!

Solutions You Can't Even Imagine!

"I will strengthen you and help you; I will uphold you with my righteous right hand."

ISAIAH 41:10 NIV

God sees solutions you cannot even imagine! After all, He is the *Creator* God. As the great I Am, He has everything under His power. Are you allowing God to work in the events of your life—or are you too busy "fixing them" to let Him into situations, and as a result blocking His way?

Allow God to lead you through the desert places. Keep your eyes on His pillar of light and follow the cloud He sends before you. Know He'll give you living water and miraculous manna along the way, continuing to take care of you until one day He leads you into the Promised Land.

God, starting today, I will allow You into my situations so You can be the "Great Fixer" in my life.

Being Still

Let be and be still, and know (recognize
and understand) that I am God.

PSALM 46:10 AMPC

Trust that everything you experience—good or bad—comes first through God, and then to you. Don't be beguiled by the darkness of doubts, what-ifs, and trials, but understand He's with you in the midst of your storms and He'll find an awesomely creative way to turn whatever evil confronts you into your eventual good.

You aren't expected to enjoy your trials, but simply understand that you must trust God's will, wisdom, and creativity, and believe that He's with you through it all until the end. Let go and let God work His marvels in good times and bad, praising Him all the way.

Help me, Lord, to be still and put the
reins of my life into Your hands.

A New Inner Woman

*You are no longer a slave, but God's
child; and since you are his child,
God has made you also an heir.*

GALATIANS 4:7 NIV

You have a choice: to either live in bondage or experience the freedom in Christ.

In the first scenario, your soul is controlled by an unyielding obligation to obey the laws of God because you fear God's punishment or expect a reward. In the second scenario, the controlling authority is a new *inner* woman who works out the will of the divine Creator without fear of being punished or for a reward. In the first, you're a slave, walking in the flesh, hoping your actions please your overseer. In the second, you're free in Christ and heir to His promises.

*Father God, thank You for
freeing me to live in You!*

Trusting Jesus

*We know that a person is made
right with God not by following the
law, but by trusting in Jesus Christ.*
GALATIANS 2:16 NCV

Even the best person can fall back into bondage by stumbling off the true path. The disciple Peter reverted back to Jewish law in an attempt to please men instead of God (see Galatians 2:12–13). But Paul, who'd confronted Peter, set people straight, telling them a person is made right with God not by following the laws but by trusting Jesus.

We're saved through our faith in Christ, and Christ alone. Anything we add to that formula is not of God and puts us in bondage.

*Thank You, my Jesus, for my
freedom in You, whom I trust!*

A Free Woman

*Now you. . .sisters. . .are children
of promise. . . . Not children of the
slave woman, but of the free woman.*
GALATIANS 4:28, 31 NIV

To their faith, the Judaizers added ceremonial law. We often add religious routines and our own egos (glorifying ourselves instead of God). Sometimes we add our Christian works, substituting them for faith. But make this clear in your mind: God is not so much interested in what you *do* as He is in what you *are*. God has His eye on your inner woman, the new creature born when you first accepted Christ. He wants you to understand that you are a free woman, not a slave (see Galatians 4:24–31).

You, Lord, have freed me! All praise to You! Amen.

Saved by Love

This is real love—not that we loved God,
but that he loved us and sent his Son
as a sacrifice to take away our sins.

1 JOHN 4:10 NLT

How exhausting to live in bondage! Thank God Christ came to save us from the law of Moses, for there was no way we could satisfy its demands. Instead, He gave us two new laws to replace all others: "Love the Lord your God with all your heart and with all your soul and with all your mind (intellect). . . . Love your neighbor as [you do] yourself" (Matthew 22:37, 39 AMPC). As we obey this law, we find ourselves walking not in the flesh but in the Spirit.

I come to You today, Lord, with love in my heart.

The Secret to Freedom

*You are no longer a slave, but God's
child; and since you are his child,
God has made you also an heir.*

GALATIANS 4:7 NIV

The secret to our freedom is to be as God sees us—as little children and heirs. Get God's view of you set in your mind. Walk as if you are a daughter of the King—because you are! "Unless you change and become like little children, you will never enter the kingdom of heaven" (Matthew 18:3 NIV). Our spiritual Father cares for us, providing everything we need and blessings besides. We needn't worry, stress, or strain about the future nor become desperate for riches other than the ones He provides in Christ.

*Loving Daddy God, help me see myself
as You see me—as a little child.*

As Little Children

[Jesus] said, "I tell you the truth, unless you turn from your sins and become like little children, you will never get into the Kingdom of Heaven."

MATTHEW 18:3 NLT

Because God has sacrificed His Son, as God's heirs we can "walk about in freedom" (Psalm 119:45 NIV), unfettered by the opinions of others—*including ourselves.* We're God's willing servants, not slaves. And because He works in us "to will and to act in order to fulfill his good purpose" (Philippians 2:13 NIV), all we need to do is accept Him as our Father, become as little children, and allow Him to take over our lives—put Him in the driver's seat. And we must not try to grab for the steering wheel, because whenever we do, we're bound to swerve off our path.

Take the wheel, Lord. You're in the driver's seat now.

Daughter of the Promises

If we live by the Spirit, let us
also walk by the Spirit.
GALATIANS 5:25 NASB

The entire key to your Christian life is to become as a little child, living and walking by the Spirit and "[not in your own strength] for it is God Who is all the while effectually at work in you [energizing and creating in you the power and desire], both to will and to work for His good pleasure and satisfaction and delight" (Philippians 2:13 AMPC). As God's daughter of the promises, having put aside all self-effort and self-dependence, you will receive "the unending (boundless, fathomless, incalculable, and exhaustless) riches of Christ" (Ephesians 3:8 AMPC).

I walk by Your Spirit, Lord.

Let the Fun—
and Joy—Begin!

*The fruit of the Spirit is love, joy, peace, patience,
kindness, goodness, faithfulness, gentleness,
self-control; against such things there is no law.*
GALATIANS 5:22–23 NASB

If we keep in mind how God views us, we will bear the fruit of His Spirit. And with our adoring eyes upon our Father—not on ourselves, others, or material things—we can relax. So rest in Daddy God. Recognize that you are His child, a beautiful daughter and heir, a free woman, a new creature in Christ. Allow His Spirit to have His way—sit back and leave the driving to Him. And let the fun—and joy—begin!

....

*In You, adoring Abba,
I rest, relax, and rejoice!*

No Failure

*You are God's garden and vineyard
and field under cultivation.*

1 CORINTHIANS 3:9 AMPC

We're all working at becoming what we believe God has called us to be. And because we're works in process, in the midst of growth, not one of us is perfect.

We can banish the grief, shame, self-doubt, and self-condemnation that come upon us when we make choices that have led us in the wrong direction. These missteps are merely part of our growth process. So take care not to succumb to constant and consistent thoughts of your failings. For as Dr. Frank Crane, minister and essayist, wrote, "There is no failure in my life. There is a lot of imperfection, but growth implies imperfection."

*Thank You, Lord, for growing me
into the woman You'd have me be!*

Growing Pains and Blessings

*"We believe that we are all saved the same way,
by the undeserved grace of the Lord Jesus."*

ACTS 15:11 NLT

As we grow up in Christ, embarking on the pathway God has marked out for us, He intends for us not to stagnate like the Dead Sea but to flow ever on to the place He calls us, nestled deep in His grace. We are not to have our flow impeded by getting hung up on our faults and failings. Instead, we can simply perceive any growing pains resulting from our missteps and imperfections as blessings, because for us who have not yet arrived, it's all about the journey.

*Help me, Lord, to see my missteps
and imperfections as blessings.*

Spiritual Growth

Grow in grace (undeserved favor, spiritual strength) and recognition and knowledge and understanding of our Lord and Savior Jesus Christ.
2 PETER 3:18 AMPC

Our joy is found in the process of our growth! And finding that joy, amid our imperfection and immaturity, is what it's all about!

We are not speaking of physical growth, because except for the skull and pelvis bones, which continue to grow throughout adulthood, our bodies eventually stop growing. (Although our ears and noses seem to grow larger, it's just cartilage breaking down and gravity taking over. Let's move on.) Here we're speaking of spiritual growth.

Show me, Lord, how to find joy as I grow in You.

Plantings of the Lord

"Your people shall all be righteous; they shall inherit the land forever, the branch of My planting, the work of My hands, that I may be glorified."

ISAIAH 60:21 NKJV

Earthly parents become alarmed and seek medical advice if their babies don't grow physically. So would God our Father be alarmed if we, His children, didn't continue to grow spiritually. Yet many of us feel as if we can accomplish this growth in our own power. Perhaps we believe that if we try to do greater and greater things, we will reach the epitome of spirituality. Yet, like the flowers and trees, we cannot *make* ourselves grow. That job has been left in the hands of our Father. We are mere plantings of the Lord—for His glory.

Thank You, Lord,
for growing me up in You. Amen.

Beyond Imagination

*Blessed is the person who...delights in
the teachings of the L*ORD*.... He is like
a tree planted beside streams.... He
succeeds in everything he does.*

PSALM 1:1–3 GW

When we feel we've not gotten anywhere, that our
lives haven't improved one iota, we may strain to
get back to the place from which we started. In this
I-want-it-now culture, we may feel discouraged if
we aren't where we think we should be in our spiritual growth. We can remedy this situation by not
attempting to grow *into* grace but endeavoring to
grow *in* grace. That means planting ourselves in
God's grace and allowing our roots to go deep into
this life hidden in Christ. Once we do, we'll grow
beyond imagination.

*I'm planting myself in Your
grace, Lord. Grow me up!*

Defining Grace

God is able to make all grace abound toward you,
that you, always having all sufficiency in all things,
may have an abundance for every good work.

2 CORINTHIANS 9:8 NKJV

How do we accomplish spiritual growth in grace? First, we need to define *grace*. It's not just God's unmerited favor, a gift He freely gives, requiring no action on our part. It's also His boundless, divine love poured out in a multitude of ways. It's an abundant, unconditional love, almost beyond human comprehension. Think of the best mother you've ever known. Take her love and multiply it by infinity, and you may have scratched the surface of God's grace to us and love for us. The only method of receiving such grace is accepting it from God's loving hand!

I accept grace from Your loving hand, Lord!

Allowing God to Be in Control

Consider the lilies of the field and learn
thoroughly how they grow; they neither toil
nor spin. Yet I tell you, even Solomon in all
his magnificence (excellence, dignity, and
grace) was not arrayed like one of these.
MATTHEW 6:28–29 AMPC

To grow in grace, our souls must be planted in the very heart of God's love. We must steep ourselves in grace and allow it to surround us. God has it in His plan that we grow in such a way. We are to consider the lilies of the field, allowing God to be in control and trusting Him to grow us as He desires, continually being open to His promptings.

Help me, Lord, to steep myself in Your
grace and become a lily of the field.

No Worries

*"Who of you by being worried can
add a single hour to his life?"*

MATTHEW 6:27 NASB

Trusting God to take care of things may be difficult for worriers. But the Word tells us not to fret or worry, because it actually impedes our growth; it reveals our doubts that God will, as promised, take care of us, just as He does His lilies. It signals to God—and others—that since we doubt His provision, we must take things into our own hands. But in doing so, we end up fighting, resisting, or impeding God's work, instead of yielding to Him and allowing Him to grow us up into the woman He wants us to be.

*Free me of worries, Lord, so that
You can do Your work in me.*

Growing Naturally

You have not chosen Me, but I have chosen you and I have appointed you [I have planted you], that you might go and bear fruit and keep on bearing.

JOHN 15:16 AMPC

To be like the lily, you must understand that *you* have not chosen Christ but *He* has chosen *you*. In fact, He's planted you! That's how you got into His grace in the first place! He's planted you as He has the lily, which revels in and responds to God's sunshine, water, and soil. The lily grows naturally. There's no stretching or straining to get something that has already been given. There's no unwarranted and fruitless toiling involved at all!

In You, Lord, I take pleasure!

The Lily's Secret

*"I will love them freely. . . . I will be like the
dew to Israel; he shall grow like the lily, and
lengthen his roots like Lebanon. His branches
shall spread; his beauty shall be like an olive
tree, and his fragrance like Lebanon."*

HOSEA 14:4–6 NKJV

Learn the lily's secret. Acknowledge that you're
planted in grace and then let God—the divine hus-
bandman—have complete control. Put yourself
in the light of the Son of righteousness, allowing
heaven's dew to quench your thirst. Be pliable and
yield to what He'd have you be!

If you expend effort trying to make yourself
grow spiritually, your fruit will bear witness to
your unnecessary toiling. You'll be burned out—a
common malady in church workers—wilting under
stress. You'll look for relief in all the wrong places
instead of to God.

*I give You complete control, Lord,
as I look to You for all things.*

A Free Surrender

He who leans on, trusts in, and is confident in his riches shall fall, but the [uncompromisingly] righteous shall flourish like a green bough.

PROVERBS 11:28 AMPC

Of course, we're not actually lilies. We're human beings with a modicum of intelligence. We have a certain degree of power and personal responsibility. Yet that's just where our hindrance to God's work comes in. Hannah Whitall Smith wrote:

What the lily is by nature we must be by an intelligent and free surrender. To be one of the lilies means an interior abandonment of the rarest kind. It means that we are to be infinitely passive, and yet infinitely active also: passive as regards self and its workings, active as regards attention and response to God.

To You and Your will, Lord, I freely surrender.

Growing God's Way

I tried keeping rules and working my head off to please God, and it didn't work. So I quit being a "law man" so that I could be God's man. Christ's life showed me how, and enabled me to do it.

GALATIANS 2:19–20 MSG

As God makes a baby grow without it even being aware that it is indeed growing, He has planted us to grow spiritually. And we are utterly helpless to do anything but allow Him control and not hinder His work within us. For when we get in His way, we expend all our energy, grow exhausted, and suddenly find ourselves growing backward rather than forward. We would be wise to tap into the lily's secret and grow in God's way.

*Show me, Lord, how to grow
in Your way, not mine.*

Be a Lily

"Blessed is the one who trusts in the LORD. . .
like a tree planted by the water."
JEREMIAH 17:7–8 NIV

If you find yourself straining to be your own gardener, refocus yourself to. . .

BE A LILY

Be careful for nothing. Pray with thanksgiving
and let God's peace reign.

Expect to bear fruit regardless of the storms,
wind, and rain.

Abide in the Vine, Jesus Christ. Open a vein
and let Him flow into your life.

Let God have His way in everything,
understanding that He'll make all things right.

Interpose no barrier to His life-giving power
working in you.

Look to Jesus, trusting Him to keep you
safe in His garden of grace and love.

Yield yourself up entirely to His control.
Say, "Yes, Lord, yes."

Yes, Lord, yes! This lily yields to You!

Servanthood

Sitting down, Jesus called the Twelve and said, "Anyone who wants to be first must be the very last, and the servant of all."

MARK 9:35 NIV

When we feel anxious, beleaguered, disdainful, exhausted, and tied up in knots about our Christian work, or when we have an impending desire to find our way out of serving others, we can be sure we have stepped off our pathway and embarked upon a route of bondage. It is then that we must immediately step back and look at our situation with the means of breaking through to receive the power that awaits women hidden in Christ.

Help me break through my anxiety, Lord, and receive from You the strength I need.

God at Work

*I will put My laws in their mind and write
them on their hearts; and I will be their
God, and they shall be My people.*

HEBREWS 8:10 NKJV

The first bondage that tells us we've stepped off our pathway is our flagging energy and will to do God's work. We feel we're no longer strong enough to accomplish what God has asked us to do. So we either do it begrudgingly or not at all. Yet God has intended us to do what He wills; He's written it upon our hearts and planted the seeds within our minds as part of His new covenant. He's working within and through you to make your work not a duty but a pleasure.

*Work through me, Lord, to make my
service to others a joy to me!*

Weakness as Strength

"My grace is sufficient for you,
for power is perfected in weakness."

2 CORINTHIANS 12:9 NASB

Your strength is your biggest weakness, because it can be a hindrance to what God wants to do through you. When a mother plays patty-cake with her infant, she picks up the baby's arms, claps his hands together, pats them, rolls them, and opens his arms for the grand finale. The baby does nothing but yield himself up to his mother's control, and Mom does it all. The yielding is the baby's part; the responsibility, the mother's. Because the child has neither skill nor capacity to do the motions to patty-cake, his utter weakness is his greatest strength, and it provides his greatest delight!

As I yield to You, Lord, work through me!

As God Wills

It is God who is at work in you, both to
will and to work for His good pleasure.
PHILIPPIANS 2:13 NASB

To break through the bondage of flagging energy and desire to do God's work, we must go to God in prayer. Ask Him to help you to understand that He has given you the energy and desire to do what He has called you to do. Envision that He is filling you up with everything you need to do the job. Recognize that your strength is your biggest weakness. "Yield yourselves unto God, as those that are alive from the dead, and your members as instruments of righteousness unto God" (Romans 6:13 KJV).

I am Your instrument, Lord.
Use me as You will.

Nurtured in the Word

Every part of Scripture is God-breathed and useful one way or another—showing us truth, exposing our rebellion, correcting our mistakes, training us to live God's way.

2 TIMOTHY 3:16 MSG

Another form of bondage is thinking we're not good enough to be serving in a particular way. We can't believe God has called us to join the worship team, serve on the church board, or head the committee for vacation Bible school. What we need to understand is that God has already gone before us and prepared the way for us. The way to break through is to build up our God-confidence by nurturing our spirits in the Word. We must read His promises, His truths, and apply them to our hearts.

Use Your Word to shape my life, Lord.

Eyes on God

And whatever you do, do it heartily, as to the Lord and not to men, knowing that from the Lord you will receive the reward of the inheritance; for you serve the Lord Christ.

COLOSSIANS 3:23–24 NKJV

A third bondage of service is doing things to exalt ourselves or with the expectation of receiving an external reward. With that kind of pressure, no wonder many Christian workers fall by the wayside. They're so anxious to do something well and right to impress people that they find themselves filled with worry. These kinds of efforts detract from Jesus. If you're exalting yourself, you've taken the glory from Christ.

The remedy is to get our eyes off "self" and back on God.

Help me, Lord, to keep my eyes on You.

Discouragement

Commit everything you do to the LORD.
Trust him, and he will help you.

PSALM 37:5 NLT

The fourth form of bondage is discouragement and despair. The outreach project that was your idea hasn't brought anyone new into church. You're ready to step down from being on the committee. This attitude indicates a lack of trust in God.

To break through discouragement, roll every care off on the Lord. Instead of giving up, lean harder on God. He'll see you through! It's the evil one who is pointing out all your faults and feeding your misgivings. Pray and trust God to give you persistence as well as the courage and care you need.

On You I lean, Lord,
knowing You'll see me through!

God's Plan for You

*"I know the plans I have for you," says the L*ORD*.*
"They are plans for good and not for disaster,
to give you a future and a hope."

JEREMIAH 29:11 NLT

To break through despair, cultivate joy within your-self. Recognize that God has a plan for your life. Take joy in that promise! Thank God for all He has done in your life already—and what He plans to do in your future. When you do, you will be so renewed that you will not be able to help expressing God-cheer! For who knows what blessings await you when you persevere!

Thank You, Lord, for planning
for my good. In You, I hope!

No Pressure

"He gave. . .to. . .each according to his ability."

MATTHEW 25:15 NIV

The sixth form of bondage is the feeling that you're doing too little or not enough. The remedy is understanding your responsibility in the matter. You're accountable for doing what God's called you to do and what He's given you the talents to perform—nothing more and nothing less. Remember that the work is God's, that He gives to each according to his [or her] skill level. What a relief that the work is God's—and you're just His instrument! You're just the chisel in the hands of the great sculptor. That truth takes all the pressure off!

Thank You, Lord, for giving me
the talents to do Your work. Amen.

God's Way and Power

*[Pray] that the Lord your God may show
us the way in which we should walk
and the thing that we should do.*

JEREMIAH 42:3 AMPC

Find rest in knowing that God will tell us the way to go, the thing to do. . .and we don't need to entertain what-if thoughts. Take on your responsibilities in God's strength, under His constant guidance, and by His leading. There's no need to be timid or worried. Just fill one sphere of responsibility, for one door opens to larger things, and another to still larger things, until you find yourself doing, in God's power, tasks you never believed or imagined you'd be doing (see Matthew 25:21). In accordance with His timing, you'll be exactly where He wants you to be.

Show me Your will and way, Lord.

Afterthoughts

This one thing I do, forgetting those things
which are behind, and reaching forth
unto those things which are before.

PHILIPPIANS 3:13 KJV

The seventh form of bondage concerns the reflections that follow the completion of any endeavor. These particular afterthoughts come in two varieties: either we congratulate ourselves upon the endeavor's success and are lifted up, or we're distressed over its failure and are utterly cast down. The breakthrough is to put the final results of any task in God's hands—and *leave them there!* Know that God is always pleased with your efforts, and move on to the next thing. Refuse to worry. Simply ask God to override any mistakes and bless your efforts as He chooses.

Lord, I leave my work in Your hands.

Blessed Endeavors

Do what the LORD wants, and he will
give you your heart's desire. Let the
LORD lead you and trust him to help.
PSALM 37:4–5 CEV

Through all your endeavors, be sure God and His will are your motivating powers. Plug into His Word to keep you fit and nourished, unfettered of stress, free of worry. Continually seek His guidance and direction through prayer; then exercise your faith by taking bold steps for God's glory and His glory alone. Know He will never give you a task without giving you the strength, courage, and means to accomplish it. Leave the results with Him, and He will bless you and all your endeavors.

Bless all my endeavors for You, O Lord.

An Epistle of Christ

If we say we are his, we must
follow the example of Christ.

1 JOHN 2:6 CEV

Although you may not be a professional preacher, your lives, words, and behavior do demonstrate to others what you believe. If you call yourself a Christian, when others see you they should also see Christ, for "clearly you are an epistle of Christ" (2 Corinthians 3:3 NKJV). Hannah Whitall Smith wrote, "The life hid with Christ in God is a hidden life, as to its source, but it must not be hidden as to its practical results."

Lord, help me follow You in all I say and do. Amen.

Seek First

*"Seek first His kingdom and His righteousness,
and all these things will be added to you."*

MATTHEW 6:33 NASB

If we're true Christians, we had best be hidden in Christ 24-7—not just when we're in the presence of other believers but *everywhere* we go and in *everything* we do!

A good place to gear up for the day's duties is early morning, setting our minds on heavenly things, not things of this earth (see Colossians 3:2), and seeking God first. In his commentary of Matthew 6:33, Matthew Henry writes, "Seek this first every day; let waking thoughts be of God. Let him that is the First, have the first."

....

Good morning, Lord! What should I do today?

The Farmer's Mule

Light, space, zest—that's GOD! So, with him on my
side I'm fearless, afraid of no one and nothing.
PSALM 27:1 MSG

One day, a mule fell into a dry well. Believing he couldn't save the animal, the farmer directed his sons to bury the beast of burden. But each time the boys threw a shovelful of dirt on top of the mule, he simply tramped on it. Soon enough dirt had come down that the mule just walked out on his own. That which was intended to bury him was the very means by which he was raised up and out of his trouble! May you be such a "mule," overcoming your obstacles and troubles instead of wallowing in an abyss of self-pity and discouragement.

Make me an overcomer, Lord!

Cultivating Joy

"With God all things are possible."
MATTHEW 19:26 NIV

Tired of trying to live up to the world's expectations? Ready for a radical spiritual transformation? You can do it—with God! Put everything you are and hope to be in the hands of the Father of lights, who has promised us "every good and perfect gift" (James 1:17 NIV). And cultivate joy for, as Henry Drummond wrote, "Joy is as much a matter of cause and effect as pain. No one can get joy by merely asking for it. It's one of the ripest fruits of the Christian life, and, like all fruit, must be grown."

Lord, all I have and all I am is in Your hands.

Endless Possibilities

The love of God has been poured out within our hearts through the Holy Spirit who was given to us.

ROMANS 5:5 NASB

You are enfolded in God's love and power. Nothing can harm you, so rest in His care. Leave yesterday with Him. He is guiding you today. And He is crowding tomorrow full of blessings and opportunities—so you have only cause for peace and expectancy. Rejoice in His safety, for you are His precious child. Know that there is nothing to fear, for behind you is God's infinite power. In front of you are endless possibilities, and you are surrounded by opportunity. Peace and power are yours in Him.

I rest in You, Lord.

Every Step

*We are God's handiwork, created in Christ
Jesus to do good works, which God
prepared in advance for us to do.*
EPHESIANS 2:10 NIV

How wonderful to be abandoned to the guidance of
our divine Master and fearlessly living our lives to
His glory. The best part is that we don't need to do
anything in our own power. He will provide all the
strength and courage we need. Our part is merely
to yield ourselves to Him; His part is to work. He
will never give us a command for which He has not
equipped us with the power and strength to obey.
He will never leave us nor forsake us. In fact, just
the opposite. . .for He always goes before us every
step of the way.

Thank You for walking with me, Lord. Amen.

Delight

My food (nourishment) is to do the
will (pleasure) of Him Who sent Me.
JOHN 4:34 AMPC

Although you don't know it yet, when you surrender yourself to Christ and obey Him in everything, you'll be fulfilling your spiritual destiny. In wholly binding your life to Him, you'll discover the reality of the almighty God! You'll be walking in light, not darkness. You'll have such an intimate relationship with the Creator that He'll tell you things that those who are further away from Him do not know! All you need to do is be totally obedient to Him, to the point where, like the psalmist, you'll declare, "I delight do thy will, O my God" (Psalm 40:8 KJV).

As I bind myself to You, Lord, help me
to fully delight in doing Your will.

The Joy of the Lord

The person who has My commands and keeps them is the one who [really] loves Me; and whoever [really] loves Me will be loved by My Father, and I [too] will love him and will show (reveal, manifest) Myself to him. [I will let Myself be clearly seen by him and make Myself real to him.]

JOHN 14:21 AMPC

This privilege of surrender isn't demanded by God; it's a matter of our choice or free will. But not abandoning ourselves to Him will keep us from having the joy of the Lord (see Luke 11:28). If we obey (or keep) His commands, we prove our love for Him. In return, Christ will not only love what we're doing, but He'll show Himself to us!

By sticking with You, Lord, I find true joy.

Our Foundation

*"I stand at the door. I knock. If you hear
me call and open the door, I'll come right
in and sit down to supper with you."*
REVELATION 3:20 MSG

Jesus is continually knocking on our doors, hoping we'll let Him in. When we do, we'll be like women who have built their houses, not upon the sand, but upon Jesus—the Rock of ages. With Him as our foundation, obeying Him and His Word every moment, we'll be able to keep our heads in times of trial. We'll keep our comfort, hope, peace, and joy amid distressing situations; we'll be kept spurred on by His amazing power! When we keep on obeying Jesus, He'll keep us safe, strong, resilient, and joyful forever!

*I open the door of my heart, mind,
soul, and spirit to You, Lord!*

Meditate on the Word

Oh, how I love your law! I meditate on it all day long. Your commands are always with me and make me wiser than my enemies. I have more insight than all my teachers, for I meditate on your statutes. I have more understanding than the elders, for I obey your precepts.

PSALM 119:97–100 NIV

Not only are we instructed to obey God and His commands diligently, but we're to meditate on them. For if we do not bathe ourselves in the Word, we'll perhaps be unclear as to what He wants us to do. The more we look to God for answers, the more we'll begin to see everything through His eyes 24-7 and keep ourselves from immediately looking to others or ourselves for direction.

Speak to me through Your Word, Lord.

Obedience and Revelation

*"And all these blessings shall come upon
you and overtake you, because you
obey the voice of the LORD your God."*

DEUTERONOMY 28:2 NKJV

God's insights are revealed to us the moment we obey. Consider Abraham. When God spoke, Abraham didn't consult his own feelings or insights or those of others but went where God told him to and did what God told him to do (see Genesis 22; Hebrews 11:17–19). When God spoke, Abraham responded, "Here I am" (Genesis 22:1 NKJV). He listened to God's request (to sacrifice his son) and did as commanded. There was no debate, argument, or questions. He simply went because God said so. Abraham obeyed, surrendered his son, and God revealed a ram as a substitute for Isaac's life. What joy obedience brings!

Here I am, Lord. I'm listening.

Don't Miss the Miracle

When He heard that he [Lazarus]
was sick, He stayed two more days
in the place where He was.

JOHN 11:6 NKJV

In a loving relationship with Christ, God may at times be silent. This is a sign of the intimacy we have with Him, like an old couple who sits quietly together, at times, comfortable in each other's silent presence. There may be a moment in which we must patiently await His next message, content with remaining with Him and meditating on His Word. If we run ahead, uncertain of His will, we may miss the miracle He is about to perform.

Abiding in You, Father, I await Your message.

His Will, His Way

*Your written instructions are miraculous. That is
why I obey them. Your word is a doorway that lets
in light, and it helps gullible people understand.*

PSALM 119:129–130 GW

Your love and devotion to Him is all the Lord asks of you as a reward for all He's done for you. So let yourself go! Lay all You have and are before Him. Pray. Bathe yourself in His Word. Ask Him to help you live out the day in His will, His way. Request His power and spiritual insight to guide you. Consciously recognize His presence in everything, and you will be brimming over with joy, lovingly embraced by this tender God, reaping the blessings of hearing His will and keeping it!

*Guide me, Lord. Open the
doorway to Your light.*

Fairy-Tale Ending

*Whoever obeys what Christ says is the kind
of person in whom God's love is perfected.
That's how we know we are in Christ.*

1 JOHN 2:5 GW

When we become Christians, we have a chance of fulfilling the happily-ever-after fairy tale with the one and only true prince—Jesus Christ. He's the One who can rescue us from the poverty of ashes and the tower of temptation. With His kiss, we're awakened to a new reality. On Him alone can we rely, for He'll never leave us. He's our comfort, peace, and Rock. He's the One with whom we want to become one and live happily ever after.

....

In You, Lord, I have my happily ever after.

All as One

"That they all may be one, as You, Father, are in Me, and I in You; that they also may be one in Us, that the world may believe that You sent Me."

JOHN 17:21 NKJV

God's entire plan for us "before the foundation of the world" (1 Peter 1:20 NASB) was for our souls and spirits to be united with our ultimate Bridegroom. This divine union is what Jesus prayed for—and not just for His disciples but for us, those who'd later come to believe in Him. This union was the mystery suddenly revealed (see Colossians 1:26). Because of Christ's death, we're right with God and can be united with Him (see Romans 6:4). It's been disclosed through the scriptures and "made known to all nations" (Romans 16:26 AMPC).

Ah, Jesus, a oneness with You is my soul's desire.

A Living Temple

Your body is a temple where the Holy Spirit lives. The Spirit is in you and is a gift from God. You are no longer your own.

1 CORINTHIANS 6:19 CEV

How wonderful to have a joy that isn't tied to our circumstances. Knowing that Christ is loving us within and sheltering us without—that no one can truly harm us—is contentment at its best.

It's also wonderful that our God never forces Himself upon us. Instead, He wants us to come to Him willingly. We're already God's living temple. Christ already resides in us, and we already received the Holy Spirit when we accepted Christ. What we need to do is continually, consistently, and completely recognize Christ's presence within us and surrender ourselves to Him.

....

I surrender myself to You, Lord.

All You Truly Need

*I have been crucified with Christ; it is no
longer I who live, but Christ lives in me.*
GALATIANS 2:20 NKJV

It's no longer we who live, but Christ who is living in us. Thus, we rely on and trust Him completely. All day and night, we steadfastly maintain this attitude, each knowing for certain this truth. And what a life with Him we will have! By surrendering all to Him, we will possess nothing—and thereby *everything!* For He is all we truly need. Fully recognizing, acknowledging, and enjoying our union with Christ, we and our prince can live together happily ever after!

You, Lord, are the only One I truly need.

Chariot of God

He makes the clouds His chariot;
He walks upon the wings of the wind.
PSALM 104:3 NASB

Often our earthly woes manifest themselves as stresses, heartaches, disputes, trials, offenses, misunderstandings, losses, and callousness. They're like juggernauts, steamrollers that wound and crush our spirits, poised to roll right over us and sink us down into the earth. But if, like Elijah, we could see these woes as God's vehicles of victory, we would rise above these cares in triumph, attaining heights we never dreamed possible! The juggernaut is the tangible, visible, earthly conveyance, whereas the chariot of God is the intangible, invisible vehicle that will take us to the heavenly places.

Raise me above my earthly woes, Lord!

Eyesight

Our lives are guided by faith, not by sight.
2 CORINTHIANS 5:7 GW

Elijah didn't fear his enemies because he walked by faith—not sight! He knew God would protect him, and that when—not *if*—he prayed, God would send His forces. If only we'd also see our worldly woes with spiritual vision, we'd open our eyes to the invisible powers of God that come to our rescue! Such "eyesight" would allow us to sit calmly within our physical houses with no fear, trusting that the intangible force of God would allow us to rise above our juggernauts in God's chariots.

Open my eyes that I may see, Lord. Amen.

Raised Up

He raised us from the dead along with Christ and seated us with him in the heavenly realms.

All the juggernauts of losses, trials, minor irritations, worries, and woes that come to us become chariots the moment we treat them as such. Hannah Whitall Smith wrote:

> *Whenever we mount into God's chariots the same thing happens to us spiritually that happened to Elijah. We shall have a translation. Not into the heavens above us, as Elijah did, but into the heaven within us; and this, after all, is almost a grander translation than his. We shall be carried away from the low, earthly groveling plane of life, where everything hurts and everything is unhappy, up into the "heavenly places in Christ Jesus" [Ephesians 2:6 KJV], where we can ride in triumph over all below.*

Raise me up in You, heavenly Lord.

Scripture Index

OLD TESTAMENT